The Rebel

OSHO FROM **FULL CIRCLE**

- Gita Darshan (Vol-II)
- Gita Darshan (Vol-I)
- Tao: The Pathless Path
- Inner War and Peace
- Die O' Yogi Die
- Behind A Thousand Names
- Freedom from the Past
- Ah This!
- The Way of the Sufi
- The Silence of the Heart
- The True Name
- The Secret
- Truth Simply Is
- In Search of Celebration
- From Sex to Superconsciousness
- Never Born, Never Died
- Walk without feet, Fly without wings...
- Won't you Join the Dance?
- Priests & Politicians – The Mafia of the Soul
- My Diamond Days with Osho
- Tantra – The Supreme Understanding
- The Goose is Out
- Sex, Money and Power
- The Rebel
- A New Vision of Women's Liberation
- I Teach Religiousness Not Religion
- Words From A Man of No Words
- First In The Morning
- Last In The Evening

OSHO

The Rebel
The very salt of the earth

FULL
CIRCLE

THE REBEL: The Very Salt of the Earth

Complied by : Annette Maxwell
Co-ordination by : Amano Surdham
Copyright © Neo-Sannyas Internationl
First Edition, 2004
First Reprint, 2006
Second Reprint, 2008
Third Reprint, New Layout, 2011
Fourth Reprint, 2015
This Reprint, May 2019

ISBN 978-81-7621-159-8

Published *by* **FULL CIRCLE PUBLISHING** *PVT LTD*
J-40, Jorbagh Lane, New Delhi-110003
Tel: +011-24621011
E-mail: contact@fullcirclebooks.in *website:* www.fullcirclebooks.in

Designing & Layout: *SCANSET*
J-40, Jorbagh Lane, New Delhi-110003

Printed at Yash Printographics, C-37, Sector-58, Noida-201301 U.P.

PRINTED IN INDIA

Contents

CHAPTER 1   The Great Synthesis   7

CHAPTER 2   The Rebel: Herald of a New Dawn   17

CHAPTER 3   Living with Your Soul on Fire   29

CHAPTER 4   You'd Better Hurry or Your Earth
             Will Be Gone   45

CHAPTER 5   Violence is Violation   55

CHAPTER 6   Society's Justice is Society's Revenge   61

CHAPTER 7   Peace Lives in Your House,
             Go Inside and Look!   77

CHAPTER 8   Existence is the Only Temple   91

CHAPTER 9   The Rebel Is A Freedom Unto Himself   103

CHAPTER 10   Ambition and Competition:
             The Pillars of Society   115

CHAPTER 11   Rebels Needed:
             Only Individuals Should Apply   131

CHAPTER 12   Rebellion: Now Or Never   141

CHAPTER 13   Your Light is the Only Right Light –
             for You   151

CHAPTER 14   Total Freedom – Nothing Less!   159

CHAPTER 15   An Enlightened Rebel Will
Shake The Thrones Of Power   171

CHAPTER 16   You Catch the Flame   177

CHAPTER 17   The Ultimate Love Affair   183

CHAPTER 18   Take Life As a Beautiful Joke   189

*Information About The Original
Audio Series*   *193*

About the Author   *194*

OSHO International Meditation Resort   *195*

Books by Osho in English   *197*

CHAPTER 1

The Great Synthesis

Beloved Osho,
How is Your rebel concerned with "Zorba the
Buddha"?

My Rebel, my new man, is Zorba the Buddha.

Mankind has lived believing either in the reality of
the soul and the illusoriness of matter, or in the reality
of matter and the illusoriness of the soul. You can divide
the humanity of the past into the spiritualists and the
materialists.

But nobody has bothered to look at the reality of
man. He is both together. He is neither just spirituality
– he is not just conciousness – nor is he just matter.
He is a tremendous harmony between matter and
consciousness. Or perhaps matter and consciousness
are not two things, but only two aspects of one reality:
matter is the outside of consciousness, and consciousness
is the interiority of matter.

But there has not been a single philosopher, sage,
or religious mystic in the past who has declared this
unity; they were all in favor of dividing man, calling
one side real and the other side unreal. This has created
an atmosphere of schizophrenia all over the earth.

You cannot live just as a body. That's what Jesus
means when he says, "Man cannot live by bread alone"
– but this is only half the truth. You cannot live just
as consciousness alone, you cannot live *without* bread

either. You have two dimensions of your being, and both the dimensions have to be fulfilled, given equal opportunity for growth. But the past has been either in favor of one and against the other, or in favor of the other and against the first one.

Man as a totality has not been accepted.

This has created misery, anguish, and a tremendous darkness, a night that has lasted for thousands of years, that seems to have no end. If you listen to the body, you condemn yourself; if you don't listen to the body, you suffer – you are hungry, you are poor, you are thirsty. If you listen to consciousness only, your growth will be lopsided; your consciousness will grow but your body will shrink, and the balance will be lost. And in the balance is your health, in the balance is your wholeness, in the balance is your joy, is your song, is your dance.

The West has chosen to listen to the body, and has become completely deaf as far as the reality of consciousness is concerned. The ultimate result is great science, great technology, an affluent society, a richness of things mundane, worldly; and amidst all this abundance, a poor man without a soul, completely lost – not knowing who he is, not knowing why he is, feeling almost an accident or a freak of nature.

Unless consciousness grows with the richness of the material world, the body – matter – becomes too heavy and the soul becomes too weak. You are too much burdened by your own inventions, your own discoveries. Rather than creating a beautiful life for you, they create a life which is felt by all the intelligentsia of the West as not worth living.

The East has chosen consciousness and has

condemned matter and everything material – the body included – as *maya,* as illusory, as a mirage in a desert, which only appears but has no reality in itself. The East has created a Gautam Buddha, a Mahavira, a Patanjali, a Kabir, a Farid, a Raidas – a long line of people with great consciousness, with great awareness. But it has also created millions of poor people, hungry, starving, dying like dogs – with not enough food, no pure water to drink, not enough clothes, not enough shelters.

A strange situation.... In the West every six months they have to drown billions and billions of dollars' worth of milk products and other foodstuff in the ocean, because it is surplus – and they don't want to overload their warehouses, they don't want to lower their prices and destroy their economic structure. On the one hand, in Ethiopia one thousand people were dying every day, and at the same time the European Common Market was destroying so much food that the cost of destroying it was two billion dollars. That is not the cost of the food; it is the cost of taking it to the ocean, and throwing it into the ocean. Who is responsible for this situation?

The richest man in the West is searching for his soul and finding himself hollow, without any love, only lust; without any prayer, only parrot – like words that he has been taught in the Sunday schools. With no religiousness – no feeling for other human beings, no reverence for life, for birds, for trees, for animals – destruction is so easy.

Hiroshima and Nagasaki would not have happened if man were not thought to be just matter. So many nuclear weapons would not have been piled up if man had been thought to be a hidden God, a hidden splendor, not to be destroyed but to be discovered, not to be destroyed but to be brought into the light – a temple of God. But if man is just matter, just chemistry, physics, a skeleton covered with skin, then with death everything dies, nothing remains. That's why it becomes possible for an Adolf Hitler to kill six million people, without a hitch. If people are just matter there is no question of even thinking twice.

The West has lost its soul, its interiority. Surrounded by meaninglessness, boredom, anguish, it is not finding itself. All the success of science is proving of no use, because the house is full of everything but the master of the house is missing.

Here, in the East, the master is alive but the house is empty. It is difficult to rejoice with hungry stomachs, with sick bodies, with death surrounding you; it is impossible to meditate. So we have been unnecessarily losers.

All our saints, and all our philosophers – spiritualists and materialists both – are responsible for this immense crime against man.

Zorba the Buddha is the answer.

It is the synthesis of matter and soul.

It is a declaration that there is no conflict between matter and consciousness, that we can be rich on both sides: we can have everything that the world can provide, that science and technology can produce, and we can still have everything that a Buddha, a Kabir, a Nanak, finds in his inner being – the flowers of ecstasy, the fragrance of godliness, the wings of ultimate freedom.

Zorba the Buddha is the new man, is the rebel.

His rebellion consists of destroying the schizophrenia of man, destroying the divisibility – destroying spirituality as against materialism, and destroying materialism as against spirituality.

It is a manifesto that body and soul are together, that existence is full of spirituality, that even mountains are alive, that even trees are sensitive, that the whole existence is both… or perhaps just one energy expressing in two ways – as matter and as consciousness. When energy is purified, it expresses itself as consciousness; when energy is crude, unpurified, dense, it appears as matter. But the whole existence is nothing but an energy field.

This is my experience – it is not my philosophy. And this is supported by modern physics and its researches: existence is energy.

We can allow man to have both the worlds together. He need not renounce this world to get the other world, neither has he to deny the other world to enjoy this world. In fact, to have only one world while you were capable of having both is to be unnecessarily poor.

Zorba the Buddha is the richest possibility.

He will live his nature to its uttermost.

He will sing songs of this earth.

He will not betray the earth, and he will not betray the sky either. He will claim all that this earth has – all the flowers, all the pleasures – and he will also claim all the stars of the sky.

He will claim the whole existence as his home.

The man of the past was poor because he divided existence. The new man, my rebel, Zorba the Buddha, claims the whole world as his home. All that it contains is for us, and we have to use it in every possible way

– without any guilt, without any conflict, without any choice. Choicelessly enjoy all that matter is capable of, and rejoice in all that consciousness is capable of.

Be a Zorba, but don't stop there.

Go on moving toward being a Buddha.

Zorba is half, Buddha is half.

There is an ancient story. In a forest nearby a city there lived two beggars. Naturally they were enemies to each other, as all professionals are – two doctors, two professors, two saints. One was blind and one was lame, and both were very competitive; the whole day they were competing with each other in the city.

But one night their huts got on fire, because the whole forest was on fire. The blind man could run out, but he could not see where to run, he could not see where the fire had not spread yet. The lame man could see that there are still possibilities of getting out of this fire, but he could not run out – the fire was too fast, wild – so the lame man could only see his death coming.

They both realized that they needed each other. The lame man had a sudden realization, "The other man can run, the blind man can run, and I can see." They forgot all their competition. In such critical moments, when both are facing death, one necessarily forgets all stupid enmities.

They created a great synthesis; they agreed that the blind man will carry the lame man on his shoulders, and they will function as one man – the lame man can see, and the blind man can run. They saved their lives. And because they saved each other's lives they became friends; for the first time they dropped their antagonism.

Zorba is blind – he cannot see, but he can dance, he

can sing, he can rejoice. The Buddha can see, but he can *only* see. He is pure eyes – just clarity and perception – but he cannot dance; he is crippled, he cannot sing, he cannot rejoice.

It is time. The world is on wildfire; everybody's life is in danger. The meeting of Zorba and Buddha can save the whole humanity. Their meeting is the only hope.

Buddha can contribute consciousness, clarity, eyes to see beyond, eyes to see that which is almost invisible. The Zorba can give his whole being to Buddha's vision – and let it not remain just a dry vision, but make it a dancing, rejoicing, ecstatic way of life.

The ambassador of Sri Lanka wrote a letter to me saying that I should stop using the words *Zorba the Buddha*... because Sri Lanka is a Buddhist country, and he said, "It hurts our religious feelings that you are mixing strange people, Zorba and Buddha."

I wrote to him, "Perhaps you don't understand that Buddha is nobody's personal property, and Buddha is not necessarily the Gautam Buddha who you have been worshiping for thousands of years in your temples. Buddha simply means 'the awakened one.' It is an adjective; it is not a personal name. Jesus can be called the Buddha; Mahavira was called, in Jaina scriptures, the Buddha; Lao Tzu can be called a Buddha – anybody who is enlightened is a Buddha. The word *Buddha* simply means 'the awakened one.' Now, awakening is nobody's property; everybody who can sleep can also awaken. It is just a natural, logical, corollary – if you are capable of sleeping, you are capable of waking up. Zorba is asleep; hence he has the capacity to be awake. So please don't get unnecessarily enraged, angry. I am not talking about your Gautam Buddha; I am talking about the pure quality of awakening. I am using it only as a symbol."

Zorba the Buddha simply means a new name for a new human being, a new name for a new age, a new name for a new beginning.

He has not replied. Even people who are holding posts of ambassadors are so utterly ignorant, so stupid. He thought that he was writing a very significant letter to me, without understanding even the meaning of the Buddha. Buddha was not the name of Gautama. His name was Gautam Siddhartha. Buddha was not his name – the name given by his parents was Gautam Siddharth. Siddharth was his name, Gautama was his family name. He is called Buddha because he became awakened; otherwise he was also a Zorba. Anybody who is not awakened is a Zorba.

Zorba is a fictitious character, a man who believed in the pleasures of the body, in the pleasures of senses. He enjoyed life to the fullest, without bothering about what is going to happen to him in the next life – whether he will enter into heaven, or will be thrown into hell. He was a poor servant; his boss was very rich, but very serious – long faced, very British.

One full moon-night.... I have not been able to forget what he said to his boss. He was in his cabin. He went outside, with his guitar – he was going to dance on the beach – and he invited the boss. He said, "Boss, only one thing is wrong with you – you think too much. Just come on! This is not the time for thinking; the moon is full, and the whole ocean is dancing. Don't miss this challenge."

He dragged the boss by his arm. His boss tried not to go with him, because Zorba was absolutely mad, he used to dance on the beach every night! The boss was feeling embarrassed – what if somebody comes and sees that he is also standing with Zorba? And Zorba was not only inviting his boss to stand by; he was inviting him to start dancing!

Seeing the full-moon night and the ocean dancing, and the tidal waves, and Zorba singing on his guitar, suddenly the boss started feeling an energy in his legs that he had never felt before. Encouraged and persuaded, finally he joined the dance, at first reluctantly, glancing all around, but there was nobody on the beach in the middle of the night. Then he forgot all about the world, and started – one with Zorba the dancer, and the ocean the dancer, and the moon the dancer. Everything became lost. It all became a dance.

Zorba is a fictitious character, and Buddha is an adjective for anyone who drops his sleep and becomes awake. No Buddhist need feel hurt.

I am giving Buddha energy to dance, and I am giving Zorba eyes to see beyond the skies to faraway destinies of existence and evolution.

My rebel is nobody else than Zorba the Buddha.

CHAPTER 2

The Rebel:
Herald of a New Dawn

Beloved Osho,
Does the rebel belong to any category?

The Rebel, by its very nature, cannot belong to any existent categories. He is a new category, he introduces a new man in the world. He is a herald of a new dawn, a new beginning. No category of the past can contain him. All the categories that have existed up to now have proved either failures, or insufficient to change the whole humanity.

The rebel is the seed for the transformation of all.

There have been great people in the world, but even the greatest of them are very small in comparison to the authentic rebel I am talking about, because they all, in some way or other, compromise with the establishment. And that's where the rebel differs from them all.

They were wise, they were creative artists, they were musicians, dancers, all kinds of people – the past has produced many luminous figures, but something is missing in them. One basic thing missing is – they all lived in a compromise with the vested interests. None of them was total in his rebelliousness. Yes, partial rebels have existed, but a partial rebel is not enough. Man needs total rebels to change the destiny of mankind from going into a graveyard, and turn its way into the garden of eden.

The rebel will have to create a category himself — by his own living, by his own responses, by his own creativity, by his own love, by his own non-compromising approach, by becoming absolutely discontinuous with the past. The rebel will not have any past, any history. He will only have the present and a vast future which is open, not dominated by the dead past, because there is no past for the rebel.

The rebel means absolute freedom, absolute love, absolute creativity. He is totally a new kind of man which has been dreamt of by a few people in the past, by a few poets, by a few philosophers, by a few mystics, but it has remained a dream — so much so that people started calling these poets and mystics utopians.

The word utopia means in its roots, "that which never comes." You can dream about it, but your dream is an exercise in utter futility; it is utopian, it is not going to come — ever. It is a hopeless hope. It is an opium to keep people dreaming and hallucinating, so that they can tolerate the suffering and misery in the present.

The rebel is not a dream.

The rebel is a reality. He is not a utopia.

He is an actual realization of man's potential, he is a promise fulfilled, a dream realized. Naturally he cannot belong to any existent category. He will have to create his own category. It will be created by the very fact that many, many intelligent people, youthful, alive, ready to take the challenge of an unknown future... slowly slowly a category will form by itself.

There are barriers for the rebel to come. The most important barrier is that he has to go against the crowd, and the crowd has all the power. The rebel is very vulnerable, as vulnerable as a rose flower. You can destroy it very easily, you can crucify a rebel without any difficulty.

But I am now feeling a tremendous guarantee that the rebel is going to be born – perhaps he is already born. People will just take a little time to recognize him. He is so new, he does not fit in any category; hence some time gap is needed to create a category and to recognize him.

Why am I so certain? I am so certain because man has come to a crisis which he has never encountered before. He has to choose either for a new man, or for committing a global suicide. And I don't think that people are going to choose a global suicide. That is my guarantee, that is my hope that the new man is bound to arise.

The days of the old man are over. It has lived too long – almost posthumously. It should have been dead long before; it has been dragging its corpse. But its time is finished. Itself it has created the situation in which only the new man, the rebellious man, rebelling against all the religions, all the governments, all the establishments, all vested interests, rebelling against all that has been keeping man blind, holding him a prisoner, forcing him to live in dark tunnels, never allowing him to know the beauties of life....

The old man has created such a situation, which was bound to happen; it was coming by and by. Each war was becoming more and more dangerous. Albert Einstein was asked, "Do you have something to say about the third world war?"

He said, "I am sorry. I cannot say anything about

the third world war, but if you want to know something about the fourth I can say."

The man who had asked the question simply could not believe that if he cannot say anything about the third, what can he say about the fourth?

He asked him, unbelievingly, "Okay, say what you can say about the fourth."

And Albert Einstein said, "The fourth will never happen – that much can be said about the fourth. About the third, nothing can be said."

All your great warriors, all your historical figures, all your so-called great men, have brought death so close that now man has to choose. There is no other alternative than a new man. The old man has erased himself out of existence.

The rebel will have a new morality – not according to any commandments, but according to his consciousness.

He will have a new religiousness; he will not belong to any religion, because that is absolutely stupid. Religiousness is a private and personal phenomenon. It is just like love, it cannot be organized. The moment you organize truth or love, you kill them. Organization functions almost like poison. The new man will not be a Christian, or a Hindu, or a Mohammedan, or a Buddhist. He will simply be religious.

Religiousness will be taken not as a belief, but as a way of life – a graceful way, a beautiful way, a responsible way, a way full of consciousness and full of love, full of sharing and friendliness, and a way of creating one world without any boundaries. No armies are needed, no weapons are needed, no nations are needed, no religions are needed.

All that is needed is a little meditativeness, a little silence, a little love, a little more humanity...just a little more, and existence will become fragrant with something so totally unique and new that you will have to find a new category for it.

The nuns in the convent were getting very restless. The Mother Superior called them together and demanded to know what was the matter. Nobody spoke until finally a new novice said, "What this place needs is some healthy males!"

The Reverend Mother was shocked. "Well, she's right. It is only human nature," another nun said boldly.

"Very well then," said the Mother Superior, "I will issue you all with candles, and you can comfort yourselves with them."

"They are no good, we have tried them," cried several voices.

"They were all right when I was young," said the Mother Superior. "What is your objection?"

"Well, Reverend Mother, you get tired of the same thing 'wick in, and wick out.'"

Man is getting tired of everything old – the old politics, the old religion, the old spirituality, the old saintliness, the old values. Man is getting utterly bored.

This century has given birth to only one philosophical school, and that is existentialism. In existentialism, boredom is the central theme – not God, not whether existence consists of matter or consciousness, not heaven and hell, not theories about reincarnation, about rebirth. The main theme is boredom.

It is not a small matter that the best thinkers of this age are finding that man's most essential need today is how to get out of this boredom that is becoming heavier and heavier, like a black cloud, and destroying all joy, making life meaningless, creating a situation in which it seems that to be born is a curse, not a blessing. The philosophers are saying that life is a curse, a meaningless boredom, an anguish unending which serves no purpose at all. You suffer so much, you sacrifice so much, and the end result is simply nothing.

The politicians have brought the nations into a state of continuous war – sometimes cold, sometimes hot – but the war continues; and the scientists have provided means to destroy this earth at least seven times. That calculation of seven times is almost ten years old. Within these ten years, they must have become able to destroy the earth at least seventy times. So many nuclear weapons!

It is a strange combination. Philosophers are giving the idea of suicide as the only way out, out of this mess, and politicians are creating communism, democracy, socialism, fascism, all kinds of ideologies – not *for* man, but man has to be sacrificed for these ideologies. And the scientists have created the right weapons in the right time, so that any moment the whole life on this planet can disappear.

I don't think it is going to happen, although preparations are complete – more than complete. It is not going to happen, because life has an intrinsic longing to live forever, to love forever, it is not desirous of death; hence the guarantee of a new man, a rebellious man, who will destroy all that which has been bringing man close to ultimate death.

The obstacles are great, but those obstacles also

have a positive side. Because they are bringing death to humanity, humanity is bound to search for a way to survive – a great rebelliousness against nations, against religions, against stupid philosophies like existentialism, against a destructive science and technology, against politicians and religious leaders who are dividing humanity, discriminating between people for no reason at all.

The new man has every chance to be the savior. Jesus is not going to come to save humanity, neither Gautam Buddha nor Krishna, but a rebellious youth around the world is going to be the savior. I trust in the young people: I trust in their longing for love, I trust in their longing for life, I trust in their longing for singing and dancing and playing music. I don't see that they are ready to die.

If the old people decide to die, they can commit suicide – nobody is preventing them. If the politicians are so much interested to die, they can jump into the ocean. But they have no right to destroy those who have not even tasted the joys of life, who have not even breathed the fragrance of existence, who have not even seen the beauty of flowers and stars, and the sun and the moon, who have not known themselves, who have not yet been travelers of their own interiority, who are absolutely unacquainted with their own subjectivity, with their own treasures.

No, the young people of the world, whatever their age... and anybody who loves life is young; even on his deathbed, if he loves life he is young. All those who are lovers of life are going to create the right atmosphere to welcome the rebellious spirit of man – because there is no other alternative.

My certainty about the rebel as the savior of man and this planet is absolute – categorically absolute. The rebel just has to be unafraid of public opinion, unafraid of the crowd, unafraid of masks, of attitudes.

A priest wanted to raise money for his church. He had been told that there was a fortune to be made racing horses, so he decided to purchase one and try his luck. However, horses were too expensive at the auction, and so he bought a donkey instead. He entered the donkey in the races, and to his surprise it was placed third. The next day the sports page in the local newspaper carried the headline, "Priest's Ass Shows."

The priest was very excited, so he entered his donkey in another race. This time it won and the papers carried the headline, "Priest's Ass Out In Front."

The Bishop was so upset with this kind of publicity that he asked the priest not to enter his donkey in any more races. Next day the papers read, "Bishop Scratches Priest's Ass."

This was too much for the Bishop, so he ordered the priest to get rid of the donkey, and the priest gave it to a nun in a nearby convent. The headlines read, "Nun Has Best Ass In Town."

The Bishop fainted. Later he informed the nun that she should dispose of the donkey immediately, so she sold it to a farmer for ten dollars. The paper faithfully reported the news, "Nun Peddles Ass For Ten Bucks."

They buried the Bishop the next day.

Just don't be worried about local newspapers, public opinion, what people say about you. These are the ways that the masses have been dominating individuals for centuries. Those who want to be themselves have not to be bothered about what the retarded masses say about them. The retarded masses have been always against any revolution, any rebellion; any change – even the smallest changes – and the masses have condemned them.

When the railway trains began for the first time, the priest, the archbishop and the pope all condemned them, saying that God never created railway trains when he created the world, so these railway trains must be the invention of the devil. And they looked like the devil; particularly the older versions of railway trains and their engines certainly looked ferocious, ugly, very evil. The churches prohibited their congregations saying, "Nobody should enter these railway trains, because the devil is going to destroy you."

The railway train was not going very far, only ten miles. For the first experiment the railway train was offering a free ticket, breakfast and lunch, a joyous journey for ten miles, and a historical experience – because nobody had ever been in a railway train, you were the first.

But then too, people who have never been regular churchgoers had gathered to listen to the bishops, to the cardinals, to the archbishop; every church was full. Those people were saying, "Don't be persuaded by the devil. Listen, he is promising you – without tickets – breakfast, lunch, a joyous journey." And they said, "You don't know – these trains will certainly start, but they will never stop." This was said by the Archbishop of England, "These trains are managed in such a way by the devil that once you enter they will start, but they will not stop – then what will you do? Just one breakfast, and one lunch, and your life is finished."

People were very afraid – on the one hand very much excited, on the other hand very much afraid. Only criminals, a few daredevils, said, "Okay, if they don't stop nothing to worry – we will see." When a few people entered then a few others, who were a little less daring, said, "If a few other people are entering, let us take a risk."

But still the compartments were almost empty; in a compartment for sixty people there were only ten people, or five people. In the whole train there were not more than one hundred people – trembling, eating breakfast, but knowing well, "This is the last breakfast, just wait for the lunch and be finished." Then this train...and it was going so fast, they had never seen anything going like that; unless the devil is driving it, such a speed is impossible.

The pope and archbishops and great Christian leaders proved to be foolish. The train came back – it stopped! But everything new, even an innocent thing like a railway train, and the masses are against it.

The masses are in the grip of the religious leaders, of the political leaders, and these people don't want any change to happen, because every change means a danger to the *status quo,* a danger to the establishment. Any change is going to bring other changes, and they will have to adjust to those changes. Who knows – are those adjustments going to be favorable to them, or unfavorable? Life *for* those leaders and the establishment is so comfortable and so luxurious it is better that everything remains the same.

But now the situation is totally different. The establishment itself has brought the situation of an ultimate change – either life or death. And the choice is such that I don't think anybody is going to choose death.

If people choose life, they will have to choose life values. Then the renunciation of religions will become out-of-date, saintliness will have to find new dimensions. Then poets and painters and singers and dancers will be the saints. Then meditators – the enlightened people, the more conscious and awakened people – will be the sages.

We are coming close to a tremendous transformation, and we are going to see it in our own lives – something so rare and unique which has never happened before and will never happen again.

You should feel fortunate, blessed, to see the great transformation of all the old values, of all the old ideals, and the birth of new values, new ideals, new categories of honor and respectability.

CHAPTER 3

Living with
Your Soul on Fire

Beloved Osho,
I find myself being deeply touched by Your vision of the rebel.
I always prided myself in being a nonconformist.
Last night in a dream I saw myself being persecuted for living rebelliously and I became afraid.
Waking up, I realized that what I used to think of as rebellion was actually a safe game for me, well within acceptable limits.
Now I see that the rebellious spirit You are talking about is something very scary, and yet something I tremendously long for.
Beloved Bhagwan, is feeling this insecurity part of becoming a rebel?

IT IS AN old association, and a misunderstanding, that to be a nonconformist is to be a rebel.

The nonconformist is a reactionary; he acts out of anger; rage, violence and ego. His action is not based in consciousness. Although he goes against the society, just to be against the society is not necessarily to be right. In fact most of the time to move from one extreme to another is always to move from one wrong to another wrong.

The rebel is a tremendous balance, and that is not possible without awareness, alertness, and immense compassion. It is not a reaction; it is an action – not against the old, but for the new.

The nonconformist is only against the old, against the established, but he has no vision of the future, no creative conception of why he is against it. What will he do if he succeeds? He will be at a loss, and utterly embarrassed. He has never thought about it. He has not felt the embarrassment because he has never succeeded. His failure has been a great shelter for him.

When I say reaction, I mean your orientation is basically dependent: you are not acting out of freedom and independence. It has very deep implications, It means your action is just a by-product; it also means that your action can be controlled very easily.

There is a small story about Mulla Nasruddin. He was a nonconformist, a fundamental reactionary, an absolutely negative mind. If his father would say, "You have to go to the right," you can be certain he would go to the left.

Soon the father became aware, and then there was no problem. When he wanted him to go to the right he would say, "Please go to the left," and he would go to the right. He was disobeying, he was nonconformist, but he was completely unaware that he was being dictated to, ordered, controlled and doing actually what his father wanted him to do.

Slowly, slowly he also became aware – "What is the matter? Before, my father used to be very angry that he had told me to go right and I went left. I am continuing to be as disobedient as ever, but now he never complains."

Soon he figured out the strategy. One day the old father and Nasruddin were both crossing the river with their donkey, and on the donkey was a big bag of sugar.

The bag was leaning more towards the right, and there was a danger that it might slip and fall down into the river.

The father was behind and he knew, "If I say, 'Move the bag towards the left,' I have got such a strange son that he will move it immediately towards the right, and the bag will fall into the river and all the sugar will be lost."

So he shouted, "Nasruddin, move the bag towards the right," hoping that he was going to move it to the left according to the old experience. But by this time Nasruddin had also figured it out. He said, "Okay," and he moved the bag towards the right and the bag fell into the river!

The father said, "What happened, are you no longer disobedient?"

He said, "Now I will decide each time whether to be obedient or not. I will not have a fixed philosophy but I will move according to the situation, because you have been cunning with me, you have been cheating me. I'm your son and still you have been cheating me! You have been ordering me in such a way that I should disobey. From today onwards be alert – I may obey, I may disobey. From today I am not going to be predictable, controllable, in your hands anymore."

The nonconformist is always in the hands of the society and the establishment. The establishment just has to be a little more clever and cunning, and then he can use the nonconformist very easily, without any difficulty.

But the establishment can never use the rebel because he is not reacting to the establishment. He has a vision of the future, of a new man, of a new humanity. He is working to create that dream, to transform it into reality. If he is against the society, he is against it because the society is a hindrance to his dream.

His focus is not on the establishment; his focus is on an unknown future, a potential possibility. He acts out of his freedom, out of his vision, out of his dream. His consciousness decides which way to go.

That is the difference between reaction and action: reaction is always determined by your enemy. Perhaps you have never thought about it, that in reaction the enemy is in a dominating position, he is deciding your action. What you are going to do, the enemy can decide.

The rebel is simply beyond conceivability to the old establishment, the rotten society and the dead humanity, because it cannot have even a fragmentary view of the great dream that the rebel is carrying in his soul. All his actions are coming out of that dream; they go against the society – but that is just a coincidence. He is not *against* the society, he is *for* a new man. His approach is positive, not negative.

He is not angry against the old society, he is full of pity and compassion. He knows how much the old man has suffered, how much and how long he has lived in misery. How can he be angry? He cannot even complain.

He is creating the new world so that this misery and this suffering and this ugly society disappears, and man can live more naturally, more beautifully, more lovingly, more peacefully, enjoying all the riches that existence makes available, all the gifts of life which are invaluable.

Freedom, love, silence, truth, enlightenment, the ultimate flowering of your being – all are available to you. The hindrances just have to be removed. All the old structures were creating more and more hindrances and obstructions against your growth. If the rebel is against those obstructions, it is to enable the new man to live without fetters, to live without imprisonment, to live outside the concentration camps and to live a life as free as a bird on the wing...as free as a rose bush dancing in the rain, in the sun; as free as a moon moving in the sky beyond the clouds in utter beauty, blissfulness and peace.

The rebel is a totally different kind of man from the nonconformist. It was good that you recognized that to be a nonconformist is not to be a rebel. Never forget it, because to be a nonconformist is very easy, but to be a rebel needs a tremendous transformation in your being.

To be a nonconformist is so cheap. Look at the punks — these are nonconformists, who have cut off their hair both sides, just keeping a small line of hair in the middle, and that too they have painted in psychedelic colors. Young men, young women...young men with half their mustaches shaved off and the other half painted, or the full mustache painted in the whole rainbow of colors — these are the nonconformists! It is very easy. You can have the buttons of your pants in the back, and you are a nonconformist. It will be a little difficult, it will need a little discipline, but it is very cheap — and very stupid, too.

A woman who is an actress and a model in Italy was sitting at the main crossroads in Rome, naked, asking people to become members of her political party. Those who were willing to become members of her political party could play with her breasts and kiss her. There was a crowd, and people standing in a row enrolling as members of her political party. Just in a single day she enrolled ten thousand people!

Now she has declared that she is going to fight the election for the membership of the parliament, and the way she is going to campaign and persuade people to vote for her, is that she will be sitting in a convertible car, naked; for whoever wants to vote for her she will stop the car, hug the man, kiss the man.

This is certainly nonconformism! She will become a member of the parliament; she can even become the prime minister of Italy if she simply tells all the members, "If you vote for me to be the prime minister of the country, I will make love to you in this very parliament hall." She is one of the most beautiful actresses in Italy, and the most beautiful model in the whole of Europe.

It is easy to be nonconformist, but what can she deliver to humanity? Her kisses won't help, neither will her tits. All this is good as a joke, but she cannot bring a blissful existence to the world, or to her own country.

The nonconformist down the ages has done every kind of stupid act. It annoys people, irritates people, but it does not help any transformation in the world. And you as a sannyasin should not be interested in this kind of circus, in this kind of stupid entertainment. You can become famous very easily...

One man in America, Robert Ripley, in the beginning of the century became world-famous in three days – and he did nothing. He just walked backwards in New York, keeping a mirror in front of him in both hands so he could see behind him, and he moved backwards. Naturally he attracted attention. Everywhere a crowd gathered; all the newspapers published his photo. He became headline news – he was the first man who had traveled backwards the whole of New York City. It became such a famous act. Finally he traveled the whole of America backwards, creating great news everywhere. People were welcoming him like a saint, and all that he was doing was carrying a mirror. It is good for a circus, but it is not going to help to bring any new values in life, any new colors, any new flowers, any new blessings to people.

It is good that you have understood it – but don't forget it.

And it is significant that the same night you had a dream where "I saw myself being persecuted for living rebelliously."

You have been a nonconformist, but you have never had any dream of being persecuted because the nonconformist at the most becomes an entertainment, a laughingstock. Who cares to persecute him? Who has time to persecute him? But just the idea, the change in your mind that real rebellion is a totally different thing, immediately brought a dream. This is significant. Your unconscious immediately warned you to be careful!

To be a nonconformist is simply an old accepted thing. It is part of the establishment and the old rotten society. Nonconformists have always existed, nobody has crucified them. They are not a danger to the society or the vested interests. It was a warning from your unconscious that you saw yourself being persecuted in a dream. "...and I became afraid. Waking up, I realized that what I used to think of as rebellion was actually a safe game for me, well within acceptable limits. Now

I see that the rebellious spirit you are talking about is something very scary, and yet something I tremendously long for. Is feeling this insecurity part of becoming a rebel?"

First, it is certainly risky, dangerous.

It is only for those who have the lion's heart, who have guts and who have the dignity of human beings.

It is not for all.

Only a few rebels are needed to create a rebellious society; the others will follow suit, but they will not, on their own, be rebellious. If the rebellious people create a society, the crowds – just as today they are part of the society – will become part of the rebellious society. But they cannot do anything on their own, for the simple reason that it is scary.

But as far as I am concerned and my people are concerned, anything that is dangerous, risky, scary, should be accepted as a challenge to your manhood, should be accepted as a challenge to your courage, to your spirit, to your very soul. It is dangerous – that's why it should be longed for.

A man who lives without danger does not live at all.

The only way to live is to live dangerously, always moving on a razor's edge. Then life has a freshness, youthfulness and a moment to moment intensity, a moment to moment totality, because the next moment is not certain at all.

Those who are living conveniently, comfortably, a middle-class life...the word "middle-class" is abusive; one should not live a middle-class life. These are the people who go on clinging to the past, clinging to corpses, clinging to rotten principles, meaningless rituals, because they are afraid even to raise a question. Their convenience is more valuable than sincerity. Their so-called middle-class comforts are more valuable to them than a life lived with intensity and fire.

A sannyasin is taking initiation to become a flame, with a longing to live dangerously, dropping all conveniences, comforts, moving always into the unknown.

But the beauty is that when you live dangerously and you don't have any certainty, any guarantee, any insurance for tomorrow, you live today to its fullest extent. You squeeze the juice of every moment to its totality, knowing perfectly well you may not have another chance.

You love, but your love is not superficial.

You live, but your life is a fire.

And even a single moment of intense love and living is more valuable than a whole eternity of futile worship, superstitions, dead ideals, slavery, bondage.

God is speaking to Moses on Mount Sinai, and Moses is shaking his head in disbelief at what God is saying to him. With his face upturned to heaven he says, "Alright, God, now let me get this straight. You are telling me that we are the chosen people, and you want us to cut the tips of our what?"

God, being a gentleman, cannot use the word. And Moses, being a prophet, also cannot use the word. So how they managed it is a mystery, because God remained silent. Perhaps it was Moses, own discovery — he had to answer to his people and he could not show his ignorance!

Jews have suffered only because of this strange idea that they accepted, that they are the chosen people of

God. This seems to be absolutely…either Moses dreamt it, or he had taken marijuana on Mount Sinai – because I know on Mount Sinai marijuana grows. But something went wrong, and he went back with the idea, "We are the chosen people." Once this got into the heads of Jews it became their ego, and nobody raised a question.

I have looked into many Jewish scriptures, old and new, into many commentators – even very logical and very significant philosophers like Martin Buber – but nobody raises any question about this stupid idea that Jews are the chosen people of God. It is so comfortable, so convenient, but it has created their whole misery for four thousand years, because nobody else will accept it.

Everybody has his own idea. Hindus think they are the chosen people of God, and that God gave to the Hindus the first holy books in the world. Hindus were the first to become a civilized nation, and they have one of the most perfect languages, Sanskrit, which they claim is the only language that God understands. So if you are praying in any other language you are simply wasting your time.

Just here in Poona, a man is teaching women for the first time in history…He thinks he is a revolutionary; he is just a nonconformist. He is teaching women Sanskrit rituals, what sutras have to be repeated in marriage, so then the woman priest can perform marriages – which has never happened in the whole of history. But the problem is that those women don't know – they are not even educated – they don't know the meaning.

The man was asked a few days ago by a journalist, "You are teaching these women these Sanskrit sutras, preparing them to be priests in temples, in marriages, in other ceremonies but they don't know the meaning." And do you know his reply? He said, "It is not a question of their knowing the meaning. God understands it, so whether they know it or not is absolutely meaningless. It is the right prayer – that I know – and it is the right prayer that God understands. The woman who is repeating it is superfluous, whether she knows the meaning or not."

He thinks he is being very rebellious! – but nobody is condemning him; people are taking it as a joke. And nobody will call those women to perform marriages. He can prepare them, and nobody will call those women into their temples to worship. He can go on preparing them – that does not matter unless temples call them to be priests, unless people start calling them for marriages, childbirth, death. That's why nobody is bothering about him. But his answer shows a great fallacy that Hindus have carried for thousands of years – that Sanskrit is the language of God, the only language he understands and the only books that he has written. And Hindus are God's chosen people; he has taken all his incarnations in the Hindu fold.

The Germans think that they are the purest race, and this was the conflict, this was why they wanted to destroy the Jews, because two peoples cannot be the chosen people of God; one has to be completely erased. When Adolf Hitler succeeded in killing six million Jews it became more and more certain to the Germans that he was right, because God was not protecting the Jews and he was not punishing Adolf Hitler either.

It is very cheap to conform to a society in which you are living, never asking any questions even if you feel that something is stupid. But just to save your convenience you are selling your soul. You are becoming a spiritual slave.

A rebel refuses to be enslaved in any way – not even by God. By man is out of the question.

Friedrich Nietzsche's statement that "God is dead and now man is absolutely free," is a statement of a rebellious soul. His argument is clear. In another place he says that "Man and God cannot coexist, because God will exist only with God as the creator and man as the created. We cannot tolerate this indignity, this insult; hence we declare that God is dead and man is supreme. Now nobody is above him."

Certainly these are dangerous paths. But those who have followed these paths have enjoyed life in its absolute glory, have lived life in utter ecstasy. Those who have remained middle-class sheep, crowds, waiting for the shepherd to come and to save them, their life is so lukewarm that it is neither hot nor cold. It is just a kind of tea which you would not like to drink – neither hot nor cold, just lukewarm.

Don't live a lukewarm life.

Harry's strong-minded wife, Martha, took him shopping to buy a pair of trousers. "Do you want buttons or zippers?" asked the shop assistant. "Zipper," replied Harry quickly.

"Very good, Sir," said the assistant, "And do you want a five inch zip or a ten inch?" "Ten inch," Harry said before Martha could interrupt.

When they got outside, Martha was furious. "You," she said, "you and your ten inch zip! Why, you remind me of the man who lives next door to my father. Every morning he goes down his garden, unlocks his garage. Opens the eight foot double doors and then wheels his bike out."

Don't live life on a bike!

What I am saying certainly creates a feeling of insecurity. But what is security? Is there anything secure in life? Does security exist at all, or is it just an idea, a consoling idea that man has created for himself? What security is there?

The people in Hiroshima and Nagasaki had gone to bed with absolute security; I don't think even a single person amongst those two big cities, two hundred thousand people, had gone to bed with any idea of insecurity. And by the morning there were only fires and dead bodies. Not a living thing was left, not even trees, not even birds, no animals, no man. All life simply disappeared. What security is there?

Do you think those six million Jews had ever thought that the gas chambers would be their end, that within a minute they would simply be going out of the chimneys as smoke in the sky? What security is there?

There has never been any security.

Death can come any moment, and it always comes without any notice, without any warning. Still we go on living with the idea of security, and whenever the idea of being a rebel, a rebellious spirit, arises, immediately we think of security.

But you don't *have* any security!

The rebel understands it: there is no security — hence, don't ask for it. Live in insecurity, because that is an actual fact of life. You cannot avoid it, you cannot prevent it, so there is no need to bother about it. Don't waste time unnecessarily.

In the days when Disraeli and Gladstone were political enemies, the British houses of parliament rang with their heated debates.

Once Gladstone shouted at the prime minister, "Sir, you will come to your end either upon the gallows or of a venereal disease."

Disraeli adjusted his monocle and replied with unruffled calm, "I should say, Mr. Gladstone, that depends on whether I embrace your principles or your mistress."

Take life at ease. Be unruffled, and move with strength and power and dignity into the unknown, into the dark, joyously, dancingly.

You have nothing to lose but everything to gain.

CHAPTER 4

You'd Better Hurry
or Your Earth Will Be Gone

Beloved Osho,
What is the difference between a rebel and a
revolutionary?

THERE IS NOT only a quantitative difference between a rebel and a revolutionary; there is also a qualitative difference. The revolutionary is part of the political world. His approach is politics, his understanding is that to change the social structure is enough to change the man.

The rebel is a spiritual phenomenon.

His approach is absolutely individual.

His vision is that if we want to change the society, we have to change the individual.

Society in itself does not exist; it is only a word, like *crowd*. If you go to find it, you will not find it anywhere. Wherever you will encounter someone, you will encounter the individual. Society is only a collective name – just a name, not a reality – with no substance. The individual has a soul, has a possibility of evolution, of change, of transformation; hence the difference is tremendous.

The rebel is the very essence of religion.

He brings into the world a change of consciousness.

If consciousness changes, then the structure of the society is bound to follow. But vice versa is not right –

and it has been proved by all the revolutions, because they have all failed.

No revolution has yet succeeded in changing man, yet it seems man is not aware of the fact; he still goes on thinking in terms of revolution, of changing society, of changing the government, of changing the bureaucracy, of changing laws, political systems. Feudalism, capitalism, communism, socialism, fascism – they are all in their own way revolutionary. They all have failed, and failed utterly, because man has remained the same.

A Gautam Buddha, a Zarathustra, a Jesus – these people are rebels. Their trust is in the individual. They have not succeeded either, but their failure is totally different from the failure of the revolutionary. Revolutionaries have tried their methodology in many countries in many ways, and have failed. But a Gautam Buddha has not succeeded – because he has not been tried. A Jesus has not succeeded because Jews crucified him and Christians buried him; he has not been tried, he has not been given a chance. The rebel is still an unexperimented dimension.

My sannyasins have to be rebels, not revolutionaries. The revolutionary belongs to a very mundane sphere. The rebel and his rebelliousness are sacred. The revolutionary cannot stand alone. He needs a crowd, a political party, a government. He needs power, and power corrupts, and absolute power corrupts absolutely.

All the revolutionaries who have succeeded in capturing power have been corrupted by power. They could not change power and its institutions; power changed them and their minds. It corrupted them. Only the names of the powerful became different...but the society continued to remain the same.

Man's consciousness has not grown for centuries. Only once in a while a man blossoms, but in millions of people the blossoming of one man is not a rule, it is an exception. And because he is alone, the crowd cannot tolerate him. He becomes a kind of humiliation; his very presence becomes insulting because he opens your eyes, makes you aware about your potential and your future.

It hurts your ego that you have done nothing to grow to be more conscious, to be more loving, to be more ecstatic, to be more creative, to be more silent, and to make a beautiful world around you. You have not contributed to the world; your existence has not been a blessing here, but a curse. You introduce your anger, your violence, your jealousy, your competitiveness, your lust for power. You make the world a war field; you are bloodthirsty, and you make others bloodthirsty. You deprive humanity of its humanness; you help man to fall below humanity, even sometimes below animals.

A Gautam Buddha or a Kabir or a Chuang Tzu hurts you because he has blossomed, and you are standing there.... Springs come and go, nothing blossoms in you; no birds come and make their nest on you, and sing their songs around you. It is better to crucify a Jesus and poison a Socrates, just to remove them, so that you need not feel in any way spiritually inferior.

The world has known only very few rebels, but now is the time. If humanity proves incapable of producing a large number of rebels – a spirit rebellious – then our days on the earth are counted, then this century may become our graveyard. We are coming very close to the point.

We have to change our consciousness, create more meditative energy in the world, create more lovingness. We have to destroy the old man and its ugliness, its rotten ideologies, its stupid discriminations and idiotic superstitions, and create a new man with fresh eyes, with new values – a discontinuity with the past. That's the meaning of rebelliousness.

These three words it will help to understand. Reform means a modification. The old remains, you give it a new form, a new shape, a kind of renovation of an old building. Its original structure remains – you whitewash it, you clean it, you make a few windows, a few new doors.

Revolution goes deeper than reform. The old remains, but more changes are introduced even in its basic structure – not only changing its color and opening a few windows and doors, but perhaps making new stories, taking it higher into the sky. But the old is not destroyed; it remains hidden behind the new. In fact, it remains the very foundation of the new. The revolution is a continuity with the old.

Rebellion is a discontinuity. It is not reform, it is not revolution. It is simply disconnecting yourself from all that is old. The old religions, the old political ideologies, the old man, all that is old – you disconnect yourself from it. You start life afresh, from scratch. And unless we prepare humanity to begin life again – a resurrection, a death of the old and a birth of the new....

It is very significant to remember that the day Gautam Buddha was born, his mother died; as he was coming out of the womb, his mother was going out of existence. Perhaps this was historical, because he was brought up by his mother's sister; he never saw his mother alive. And now it has become a traditional idea in Buddhism that whenever a buddha is born, his mother dies immediately, his mother cannot survive. I take it as a symbolic and very significant indication: it means the birth of a rebel is the death of the old.

The revolutionary tries to change the old. The rebel simply comes out of the old, just as the snake slips out of the old skin – and never looks back. Unless we create such rebellious people around the earth, man has no future.

The old man has brought man to his ultimate death. The old mind, the old ideologies, the old religions – they have all combined together to bring this situation of global suicide. Only a new man can save humanity, this planet, and the beautiful life of this planet.

I teach rebellion, not revolution.

To me rebelliousness is the essential quality of a religious man. It is spirituality in its absolute purity.

The days of revolution are over. The French revolution failed, the Russian revolution failed, the Chinese revolution failed, and in this country we have seen with our own eyes the Gandhian revolution failed – and it failed in front of Gandhi's own eyes. Gandhi was teaching nonviolence his whole life, and before his own eyes the country was divided; millions of people were killed, burned alive, millions of women were raped and Gandhi himself was shot dead. That is a strange end for a nonviolent saint.

And he himself forgot all his teachings. Before his revolution had succeeded, he was asked by an American thinker, Louis Fischer, "What are you going to do with arms, armies, all kinds of weapons, when India becomes an independent country?" And Gandhi said, "I'm going to throw all the arms into the ocean, and send all the armies to work in the fields and in the gardens." And Louis Fischer asked, "But have you forgotten? Somebody can invade your country." Gandhi said, "We will welcome him. If somebody invades us, we will accept him as a guest and tell him, 'You can also live here, just the way we are living. There is no need to fight.'"

But he completely forgot all his philosophy. That's how revolutions fail. It is very beautiful to talk about these things, but when power comes into your hands.... First Mahatma Gandhi did not accept any post in the government. It was out of fear, because how is he going to answer the whole world? What about throwing the arms into the ocean? What about sending the armies to work in the fields? He escaped from the responsibility for which he had been fighting his whole life, seeing that it was going to create tremendous trouble for him; he would have to contradict his own philosophy.

But the government was made up of his own disciples, chosen by him. He did not ask them to dissolve the armies; on the contrary.... When Pakistan attacked India he did not say to the Indian government, "Now go to the borders and welcome the invaders as guests." On the contrary, he blessed the first three airplanes that were going to bomb Pakistan. With his blessings...the three airplanes came down over the villa house where he was staying in New Delhi, and he came out into the garden to bless them. With his blessings they went ahead to destroy our own people, who just a few days before were our brothers and our sisters. Unashamedly, without ever seeing the contradiction....

The Russian revolution failed before the very eyes of Lenin. He was preaching according to Karl Marx that when the revolution comes we will dissolve marriage because marriage is part of private property, and as private property goes out, marriage will also go out. People can be lovers, can live together; children will be taken care of by the society.

But as the revolution succeeded, he saw the enormousness of the problem. To take care of so many children – who is going to take care of those children? And to dissolve marriage.... For the first time he saw that society depends on the family. Family is a basic unit; without the family your society will be dissolved...it will be dangerous to create a dictatorship of the proletariat, because people will become more independent if they don't have the responsibilities of the family.

You see the logic: if people have the responsibilities of a wife, of an old father, an old mother, of children, they are so burdened that they cannot be rebellious. They cannot go against the government – they have too many responsibilities. But if people have no responsibilities, if the old people are taken care of by the government as they had been promising before the revolution, if children are taken care of by the government.... If people are living together as long as they love each other, they don't need permission for marriage and they don't need any divorce. It is their private, personal affair and government has no business to interfere.

When it came about that the power was in the hands of the Communist party and Lenin was the leader, everything changed. Once power comes into their hands, people start thinking differently. Now the thinking was that to make people so independent of responsibilities is dangerous – they will become too individualistic. So let them be burdened with a family. They will remain enslaved just because of an old mother, an old father, a sick wife, children and their education, and they won't have either the time or the courage to go against the government in any matter.

Family is one of the greatest traps the society has used for millennia to keep man a slave. Lenin forgot all about dissolving families....

It is very strange how revolutions have failed. They have failed at the hands of the revolutionaries themselves, because once the power comes into their hands they start thinking in different ways. Then they become too attached to the power, and their whole effort is how to keep the power forever in their own hands and how to keep the people enslaved.

The future needs no revolutions.

The future needs a new experiment which has not been tried yet – because although for thousands of years there have been rebels, they remained individuals. Perhaps the time was not ripe for them. But now the time is not only ripe...if you don't hurry, time has come to an end.

By the end of this century either man will disappear, or a new man with a new vision will appear on the earth.

He will be a rebel.

CHAPTER 5

Violence is Violation

Beloved Osho,
Can You please say something about violence as the
expression of rebellion?

VIOLENCE CAN NEVER be a part of the rebellious
spirit, for the simple reason that violence is the whole
past of humanity – and the rebel wants to discontinue
with the past. Violence has been the way of life for
millennia. Directly or indirectly we have lived under
violence. Our armies, our police, our jails, our judges,
our wars, our so-called great religions, all have lived
in violence. And violence, reduced to its essentials, is
irreverent towards life.

To me the religious man, the religious consciousness,
is nothing but a deep reverence for life itself, because
there is no god beyond life, there is no paradise beyond
consciousness. Violence is a violation of both life and
consciousness. It is destructive.

The rebel is a creator; his whole philosophy is that
of creativity. We have lived in destructiveness far too
long, and what is the achievement? That's why I have
made a clear-cut distinction between the rebel and the
reactionary. I have also made a distinction between the
rebel and the revolutionary.

The reactionary is the lowest category. He can never
disconnect himself from the past. Past is his orientation,

he reacts against it. But whether you are for it or against it, it remains your reference, your context.

The revolutionary is a little higher than the reactionary. He does not only react, he also has dreams of the future, he has his utopias. But as far as violence is concerned, the revolutionary down the ages has thought that right ends can be attained through wrong means.

I refute that contention. Right ends can be achieved only through right means. Through violence you cannot achieve a peaceful, silent, loving humanity. The violence will be in the roots, it will poison your whole super-structure.

The rebel has to be nonviolent, out of sheer necessity.

Unless he is nonviolent, he cannot be the vehicle of a peaceful, warless, classless humanity.

If you sow the seeds of violence, you cannot expect and hope that the flowers will not be affected by violence. Those flowers will come out of the seeds you have sown. So each violent revolution has created another violent society, another violent culture. It is disgraceful to see that we still need armies, that we still need nuclear weapons. It is undignified to see that we need the policeman, the court and the jail. A better humanity, a more conscious man, will get rid of all this nonsense that surrounds us and pollutes our whole being.

The rebel cannot be half-hearted. He cannot be a chooser; he cannot choose a few things from the past, and not choose a few other things. Past as a whole has to be completely denied. Only then can we get rid of barbarousness in humanity, cruelty, violence and a deep-rooted disrespect for life and existence.

My approach is that of reverence for life.

The rebel will be ready to die, but he will not be ready to kill. It is the pride of man to die for a cause. It is animalistic to kill someone, however great the cause may be. By killing, you have spoiled it completely. And looking practically, the rebel is an individual against the whole world; even if he chooses to be violent, he will be crushed. The enemy – the past – has much more violent powers in his hands.

The rebel has to trust in love, has to trust in meditativeness, has to be aware of his immortality – that even if his body is crucified he remains untouched. Here I am not talking only about the political rebellion. I am talking about the individual rebel – a spiritual phenomenon, not a political entity. And no spirituality can accept violence as a means to attain the end.

Violence is simply out of question as far as my rebellion, my rebel, is concerned. He cannot destroy – we have destroyed enough. He cannot kill – we have killed enough. It is time to stop this whole idiotic way of life. We have to come out of this darkness into the light. Even if it costs you your life it is perfectly good... because my rebel will be basically a meditator.

I am not conceiving my rebel without meditation; that is his essential experience. And once you understand that you are immortal, who is worried about being killed? And if millions of meditators are ready to open their chests before the guns of the old and the rotten past, there is a possibility: perhaps it may also bring a change of heart in those people who have these destructive weapons in their hands.

Rebellion has not been tried on a vast scale. Just with the effort of millions of people meditating, loving silence and peace, and destroying all kinds of discriminations which create violence, we will be making the space, the gap, the discontinuity that can save man, and life on this planet.

CHAPTER 6

Society's Justice is
Society's Revenge

Beloved Osho,
What is justice for a rebellious man?

IT IS ONE of the most significant questions to be asked – for the simple reason that the outgoing man has never tried to remove the causes of injustice. On the contrary it has been, in the name of justice, taking revenge on the individuals who were not obedient to the social order, to the establishment, to the vested interests. They were condemned as criminals, punished – and it was thought that justice had been restored.

In fact, the people who had been punished were really the victims.

Justice was not restored. In fact, the people who were the root causes of injustice in the world had taken their revenge. Their revenge was fulfilled, and people were made afraid not to go in any way against the social order.

It is very strange that a long history…and nobody has tried to look at why injustice exists at all. We have been trying only individuals, and they are not the causes, only symptoms.

For example, a poor man is forced to steal in certain circumstances. If you really want justice to be restored, his poverty should be removed. But no, you throw the poor man into jail for a few years, and you create more injustice in the society – because then his children are bound to become beggars, or pickpockets, his wife is bound to become a prostitute. And the man you have jailed for a few years – you have taken away his humanity, his pride, his self-respect; you have humiliated him so much that back in the society he will find himself a stranger whom nobody trusts, who cannot get a job, whom everybody avoids. Nobody wants a friendship with him. He is again forced to steal.

It is a known fact that once a man is forced into jail as a punishment, he automatically comes again and again to the jail. In the long run, the jail becomes his home, he becomes a jailbird. The outside world is just a holiday resort. Just once in a while he is out in the world – but the world is not accepting of the man, does not treat him on equal terms as it treats other human beings. Insulted, he also becomes revengeful.

Revenge cannot create anything else except revenge. Hate creates more hate, revenge creates more revenge. In the jail he becomes more and more an expert. He is no longer an amateur – the first time he was an amateur. In the jail, which almost should be named as a university for crimes, a teaching school, a productive field for criminals...in the jail he learns that it is not the crime that is punished, it is being caught that is punished. Don't be caught – and you have not committed the crime. There are senior experts in the jail; they teach the novice, they initiate him into the secrets of the criminal world. Each time he comes out of the jail, he is more mature as far as crime is concerned.

But perhaps the old humanity was not interested in removing crime completely. It was only interested in punishing the disobedient, the unfit – those who wanted to go on their own way, those who did not want to become a cog in the wheel, those who had a certain individuality. There was no other avenue open for them, except crime. Crime was their sort of rebellion.

The rebellious man and his world will look into the causes. No man is born as a criminal; every man is born as a sage, innocent. It is a certain kind of nurturing, a certain kind of society, a certain upbringing, that reduces him into a criminal.

The society of the rebels will remove the causes. For example, poverty will not be allowed on the earth. And once poverty is removed, almost fifty percent of crimes will be removed, and fifty percent of judges, fifty percent of courts, fifty percent law – enforcement authorities, and fifty percent of laws – just by removing poverty.

Secondly, now science is absolutely certain that there are crimes which are hereditary. You are unnecessarily punishing a person – he needs sympathy, not punishment. For example, a rapist...in a Mohammedan country this crime is thought so big that death is the only punishment. But rape can be removed completely.

In any aboriginal society rape does not exist because young children, the moment they become aware of their sexual energy and the upsurge of sensuality, are not allowed to live in their parents houses. They have a hall in the village; all the young people live in that hall. They come in contact with all kinds of girls and all kinds of boys; they are allowed absolute sexual freedom, with only one condition – which seems to be very significant – that you can be with a girlfriend or a boyfriend only for three days; then you have to change. This gives a chance for everybody to experience everybody else, and also it gives an immense opportunity to drop jealousy. It is absolutely impossible to be jealous because your girlfriend is now moving with somebody else. There is no fixed relationship; only for there days you can be together, then you move on, change.

By the time they are of marriageable age, they are so experienced about every girl of the tribe and every boy of the tribe that they can choose the right partner, with whom they are in the most harmonious relationship. Strangely enough, in such a licentious society there is no rape – never recorded in the whole history of mankind – and there is no divorce either. They have found the right person because they have been given the opportunity. Their love goes on growing, their harmony becomes richer and richer each day.

In aboriginal societies divorce is unknown, adultery is unknown – not that they have any commandments, but by the simple fact that everybody has known everybody else in the tribe, and after this knowledge and experience they have chosen their partners. Parents don't arrange marriages; the young people choose for themselves.

In a rebellious society, the same will be the pattern. And particularly after the invention of the pill, it is absolutely absurd that a man has to marry a woman he has not known intimately or a woman has to marry a man she knows nothing about. The pill should have been a great revolution. But all the religions are preventing that revolution. They think the pill is an invention of evil forces; it should not be used.

The old pill was only ninety nine percent reliable

because sometime one could forget to take it. Now, two other pills have come into existence. One a woman can take after making love, so there is no question of any loopholes; secondly, another pill has come into existence which the man can take – no need for the woman to take any pill.

With these pills available, men and women can experiment until they come to a person with whom they would really love to be for ever. And they need not be in a hurry and rush to the church, they can wait. For a year or two they can see how their intimacy goes, whether it goes deeper and becomes richer, or whether as time passes it fades away. Before deciding for a life partner, this seems to be simply logical – to experiment, to experience as many people as possible. Adultery will disappear, rape will disappear.

And science will find, as we have already been finding, that there are crimes which a man is committing under biological laws – he is forced to commit them by his heredity. Then he needs hospitalization, medical care; or, if he has something wrong with his mind, then he needs a psychiatric hospital. But there is no question of calling him a criminal and there is no question of giving him any punishment.

All punishment is crime.

Just because we have not been able to find the causes...or perhaps we were not willing to find the causes, because to find the causes will mean changing the whole social structure, and we were not ready for that great revolution.

The rebellious man is ready for every revolution in every area of life. Injustice disappears…and there is no question of any justice.

It is very difficult to conceive a man without jealousy, a man without anger, a man without competitiveness, a man without a lust for power, but it is all possible. We have just never thought about how to remove the causes.

Why do people want power? Because whatever they are doing is not respected. A shoemaker is not respected like the president of a country. In reality, he may be a better shoemaker than the president is a good president. The quality should be praised – if a shoemaker is a better shoemaker, then he need not be interested in being a president. His own art, his own craft, will bring him dignity and the respect of the people.

It actually happened – because Lincoln's father was a shoemaker, and Lincoln became the president. The whole American aristocracy was very much shocked that they had to live under a shoemaker's presidency. In the Senate there were all aristocrats – super-rich people. The first speech that Lincoln delivered on the inauguration of his term was interrupted just in the beginning by a man, very arrogant and egoist, standing up and showing his shoes and saying, "Mr. Lincoln, by accident you have become the president. But never forget that your father was a shoemaker. In fact, in my family your father used to come to make shoes for everybody. The shoe I am showing you is made by your father."

The whole Senate laughed; they thought they had humiliated Lincoln. But it is difficult to humiliate people like Lincoln. There were tears in his eyes, and he said, "I am immensely grateful to you for reminding me of my father. He was a perfect shoemaker, and I know I cannot be *that* perfect a president. I cannot beat him. But I will try my best at least to reach closer to his greatness.

"As for your family and the shoes my father has made, I can inform the whole Senate that there may be other aristocratic families that my father used to make shoes for. A little bit of shoemaking art he has taught me too. If his shoes are not working well – if they pinch you, if they are too tight, or too loose – I can always mend them. I am my own father's son. Never feel embarrassed – just inform me. I can come and do my best. Of course, it will not be the same as my father, but he is dead."

There was great silence…the senators could not believe – what mettle is this man Lincoln made of? You cannot insult him. He can turn your insult into great respect. And he is so humble, how can you humiliate him? Only arrogant people can be humiliated.

A commune where rebellious people live will be non-competitive, will give equal opportunity to everybody to be himself. It will accept everybody the way he is.

And all are needed – the shoemakers, and the toilet-cleaners, and the presidents – all are needed. In fact, there may come a time when there will be no need of presidents, no need of prime ministers, no need of government itself; but there will never come a time when there will be no need for a shoemaker or a toilet-cleaner. They are far more essential, they serve society in a more fundamental way. All respect is due to them.

When everybody is respected as he is, his profession is respected, whatever it is, you are cutting the very roots of crime, of injustice. And when there is no money as an agency for exchange, nobody can become richer and nobody can become poorer.

The miracle of money is that it can be accumulated. You cannot accumulate wheat. How much can you accumulate? – it will get rotten. You cannot accumulate flowers, you cannot accumulate milk products, how much can you do that? You have to share them, and you have to be quick to share them – because the fresher they are, the better. The currency note never gets old and the currency note never gets rotten. You can go on collecting currency notes. The division of classes in the society between the poor and the rich is because of the currency notes.

The rebel will remove all currency, all money.

Everybody should get his needs fulfilled. The commune will be responsible to take dare. The commune will make every effort to be richer, to be healthier, to live more comfortably, to live more luxuriously. But for that you don't need a great bank account, and you don't need to reduce thousands of people to starvation.

The rebel will look at every problem of life from its very roots. He will not repress the symptoms, he will destroy the causes. And if all the causes of injustice are destroyed, then justice is restored for the first time.

Right now, we are all living under injustice, multi-dimensional injustice. And to keep this injustice prevailing, we have armies, we have police, we have national guards and we have courts, and we have judges. This whole profession is absolutely useless! All these people should be taught some craft – shoemaking, weaving clothes, carpentry. If they cannot do anything very skillful, then unskilled labor – they can at least carry bricks, participate in the construction of houses and roads. At least all your judges and all your great law experts can become gardeners.

But the whole department of justice is to protect so many injustices that are in existence, and the people who are in power want those injustices to continue.

The world of my vision – the world of the new man – will remove all causes. Many crimes – murder, rape, even stealing – are hereditary. You need your chemistry to be changed, your hormones to be changed.

A few crimes are because you have a wrong psychology; you need a good brainwash, and more clarity of vision. And all this should not be considered as punishment. If somebody is suffering from tuberculosis you send him to the hospital, not to the jail, and to be in the hospital is not considered to be criminal. And once you are healthy, and back in the society, your dignity is not destroyed.

There are many problems which have not even been touched by the old man. They have been avoiding them, postponing them. Their greatest fear was that the powerful people were one of the causes of all the crimes, that the rich people were a cause of all the crimes, that the priests were a cause of all the sexual crimes, sexual perversions, homosexuality, lesbianism. They never brought those causes to light....

Now all the governments all over the world are concerned about AIDS, and many governments have decided that homosexuality is a crime, punishable at least by five years of jail. Now this is so stupid, one cannot consider humanity to be behaving intelligently, because the jails are one of the places where homosexuality thrives. In American jails they had a survey made, and thirty percent of inmates have confessed that they are practicing homosexuality. And if thirty percent are confessing, the percentage of real homosexuals is bound to more – maybe fifty percent, maybe sixty percent.

Now homosexuality is to be condemned as a crime, and homosexuals will go underground. Right now they have their own clubs, their own restaurants, their own discos, their own gay bars. They will have to go underground, and they will become more dangerous because they will not accept that they are homosexuals.

It is almost an impossible task to test five billion human beings to know who is suffering from AIDS and who is not. Just in Texas, when they passed the law that homosexuality should become a crime punishable at least by five years of imprisonment, thousands of homosexuals protested against the Assembly Hall. Nobody would have thought that Texas – a very backward state in the United States, a desert – has so many homosexuals...and it must have more, because these were only the protesters; many may not have come to protest, because that declares that you are a homosexual.

If this is the situation in Texas, what about California? Perhaps in California it is difficult to find someone who is *not* a homosexual. There is no need to give any imprisonment. Just raise a big wall around the whole state of California, why bother about sending single individuals to jail? And there are millions of lesbians all over the world.

The real culprit is religion, which has been teaching people to be celibate. It is celibacy that has created homosexuality. Celibacy should be condemned as crime, punishable.

But these are the people who are in power – the priests, the pope, the shankaracharyas, the jainacharyas, the presidents like Ronald Reagan. They are all fanatically religious. And to see that celibacy is the cause needs a little more intelligence. Any idiot can be a fanatic – in fact, only idiots can be fanatic. An intelligent man is not fanatic, there is no need. He has arguments and evidences and reasons for whatever he does; whatever is his way of life is based on experiments and intelligence, not on a fanatic attitude.

The future man will destroy all the causes of injustice. And if something comes to a man from heredity, that is a very simple matter of changing hormones, changing your chemistry, your physiology. If something is in your mind, that too can be operated upon. You will be surprised to know that your mind has seven hundred centers, and these centers control everything in your life – hunger, thirst, sensuality, sexuality – everything. If something is wrong in those centers, if they are malfunctioning, they can be put right. Now brain surgery is in a position to know exactly which center controls which act. With the collaboration of science, psychology, psychoanalysis, psychiatry, the rebel will be able to remove all injustice, and the very question will become irrelevant.

You are asking, "What is justice for a rebellious man?" To destroy all the causes of injustice…to help people to be healthier, to be more sane, to change their chemistry so their anger, their violence, disappear; to give everybody the same respect as anybody else has –

because everybody is helping the society to be beautiful and to be richer, is helping life to be meaningful and significant, and they all should be rewarded with honor.

Then politics will disappear automatically, lust for power will disappear automatically. If there is no money to steal, stealing will disappear automatically. If everybody's need is fulfilled, then people are not mad to go on stealing unless they are suffering from something – for example, kleptomania.

I had one professor who told me, "You have to do something about my son."

I said, "What is the matter?"

He said, "Everything is right, but he is a kleptomaniac, he steals things. He does not need them, so it is not a question of need. He steals useless things, just one shoe – now, what are you going to do with one shoe? – any kind that he can manage. And he keeps them all in a cupboard, labeled – date, from whom."

I made friends with the boy. He was only fourteen; that is a vulnerable time, because one becomes sexually mature. And his father was a very-very religious type; he would not allow his boy to have any friendship with any girl. I watched the whole situation.

I said, "I would like to see your collection."

He said, "Really? – everybody condemns me for my collection. You have given me the right word. It is a collection; they say it is stealing."

I said, "No, why it should be stealing? You don't need anything; you have everything that you need. It is a beautiful collection, and it shows your intelligence – how many people you have been cheating."

He said, "You are my man."

"You just take me to your collection."

He opened the doors. It was full of all kind of junk. He had taken away some body's cycle seat – there was no need, what can he do with that cycle seat? And when I saw one shoe, I said, "Where is the other?"

He said, "I have left it there, because I don't need shoes, and anyway they are not my size."

"But why have you brought this one?"

He said, "That professor thinks himself a great genius. You know the professor of botany – so arrogant – he had brought new shoes that very day. I had to hang out for hours around his house, so that when he went out...the moment he went out I took away one shoe, and since then he has been searching for his new shoe. I never allow anybody to see my collection. You are the first."

I said, "It is a historical collection." I saw a few buttons, half a fountain pen, somebody's hat; he had slips attached to them – the name to whom the hat belongs, on what date it has been taken away from the owner.

I talked with his father. I said, "He is not a thief, because in his whole collection there is not a single thing of any use. He simply wants to do something. He has too much energy, and you don't allow any outlet for him."

He said, "What do you mean?"

I said, "Just let him find a girlfriend."

He said, "You will corrupt him."

I said, "I am going to *correct* him! You are corrupting him. Just give me a chance; otherwise he will turn into a great thief in his life, and he will forget completely for what purpose he has started all this."

And once he got a girlfriend, he stopped stealing things. One day he asked me, "What do you think? I would like to return this collection to their owners because it is unnecessary."

I said, "That will be a great joy. They will also enjoy it. You simply go distributing things from wherever you have collected them."

He said, "I have got everything recorded."

One has to look into the cause of why something is happening – why a man has been murderous, why a man has been suicidal, why a man has been a thief, why a man has been committing all kinds of crimes.

There must be causes which can be removed.

Once the society is no longer under a power block – the politicians, the priests, the capitalists – all causes can be removed. People will completely forget the word "justice," because there will not be any justice or injustice in existence.

There is one tribe in Burma, a very small tribe, whose whole history is a great example of what I am saying. There has never been any murder, there has never been any suicide, there has never been any rape, there has never been even fighting.

The simple reason is that for centuries they have practiced something of a deeper psychoanalysis than Sigmund Freud knew. Everybody, has to tell his dream in the morning. Most of the people don't dream, because there is no repressive order; without repression, dreams cannot exist. But once in a while somebody dreams that he has slapped somebody else – it is a small tribe, everybody knows everybody else. Then he has to go to that person with sweets and fruits and flowers and ask his apology, "Forgive me, in my dream I slapped you."

It looks very crazy, but whether you slap somebody when you are awake or you slap somebody when you are asleep, is there any difference in your action? It is the same action. Perhaps you wanted to slap him while he was awake and you were awake, but you somehow repressed the desire; perhaps he is stronger than you – hence the dream. But you have to go to give him fruits and sweets, and ask his apology. And unless he forgives you, you have not to leave his door.

That society has livep in such peace for centuries. If it can happen in one tribe, it can happen on the whole earth – because man is the same.

Justice will be just the very natural thing. Once in a while something will go berserk, but that does not need punishment; it needs help, it needs love, it needs compassion. The source needs to be found – why did it happen? That man has to be put in a psychiatric hospital and taken care of, with great respect. And when he is back, he is to be welcomed – he is cured.

All crime is illness, sickness. It does not need any punishment; it needs understanding, and it needs treatment.

CHAPTER 7

Peace Lives in Your House, Go Inside and Look!

Beloved Osho,
What is peace for the rebdlious man?

PEACE IS, FOR the rebellious man, his very light. It is his very aroma, his fragrance, the harmony of his heart, his at-oneness with existence. All conflicts of the mind are just memories of the past. The mind is no longer divided, split or schizophrenic. The mind has become an organic unity.

The ordinary man who has not tasted rebellion or religion – which, to me, are equivalent – is a house divided against himself. He is continuously fighting within and without. He is fighting for money, for power, for prestige, for respectability. His outside life is nothing but power politics. It is a continuous, ongoing warfare, that ceases only when he stops breafhing.

The inner scene is not much different either, because the outer and the inner cannot be much different. They are part of one individual – the outside and the inside. Inside he is struggling against nature, his own nature. his own instincts, which some so-called wise men have condemned. He is blindly following their condemnation without any understanding of his own. Fighting with his own nature, he becomes crippled.

The man who is fighting against his instincts – that is his body – is bound to fight against his intuition, which is his very soul. The man who cannot find peace with his body cannot hope to find peace with his soul, because to find peace with the body is simple; to find peace with the soul is more subtle, more invisible.

The man is fighting with his full force against every inclination that existence has given to him – against his love, against his longing for truth – because the traditionals go on teaching him, "You need not search for truth; it has already been found. You simply believe in it. From your side any search is a sign of revolt. You simply have faith, faith in Jesus Christ, faith in Mahavira, faith in Gautam Buddha...." but neverfaith in yourself.

All the religions are agreed on one point: that you should not trust yoursdf. You should be constantly conscious and alert against yourself. They have made you an enemy of yourself; hence, every moment a subtle underground struggle and conflict goes on within you. There is neither peace inside, nor is there peace outside.

Yes, sometimes you say, "I am living peacefully," and sometimes you say, "I am feeling very upset." But the difference between your peace and your being upset is not of quality but only of quantity, of degrees. What you call peace is cold war. You are tired, exhausted; there is a limit to everything. You need a little rest to be ready to start the old game again. So sometimes you are in a state of cold war within and without, and sometimes you are in a hot war within and without. But the war continues; whether it is cold or hot makes no difference.

You are never at peace, you cannot be. You have not prepared the ground for the flowers of peace to blossom. You don't deserve it. Although you have the potential, although you could be worthy. you are not worthy – and remember the difference. It is within your hands, it is within your reach, but you have not even looked at it. You are looking away from it, at everything that disturbs it.

Diogenes, one of the most peaceful men the world has known, had asked Alexander the Great, who had come to see him, "Where are you going? What is your goal? What do you really want? For months I have seen all these armies passing by, and I go on wondering what could be the purpose of it all." And Alexander said, "I want to conquer the world."

Diogenes said, "Agreed, so then you have conquered the world. accepted – then what?"

Alexander felt a little embarrassed. Nobody has asked such a question in such a manner. But still he said politely, "Then I will relax."

Diogenes laughed a belly laughter; the whole valley resounded with his laughter in the early morning. He looked at his dog. He had only one companion, a dog; they used to live together, they lived their whole life together. He looked at the dog and said, "Have you listened? Do you understand?" And Alexander could not believe that the dog nodded his head showing, "Yes, I understand."

Alexander said, "I am amazed. What does he mean by nodding his head that he understands?"

Diogenes said, "The whole existence understands that if you really want to relax, who is preventing you? Why waste time in conquering the world? You are talking as if to relax, to be peaceful, to be meditative, to be silent, to enjoy the morning sun and the cool breeze, one first needs to conquer the whole world. Then peace will be very difficult. What about us poor people who have not conquered a single thing, who do not possess a single thing? But I am already relaxed, I am at peace, I am enjoying this moment to its fullest. And we have enough space" – there was the whole bank of a river, a wild river.

He said, "You can take any place; you choose. Here there is no question of conquering or invading. If you want this place where I am lying down, I can move a little, you can take it. If you want my dog's place he can move, he is very understanding; he is no ordinary dog, he is a dog who has come to experience peace. That's our bondage, our friendship, our love, our brotherliness. I don't like to be in crowds of men because tbey don't understand a thing. I like my dog, he is so understanding." And the dog really moved away, wagging his tail and welcoming Alexander , "You can take this place."

Alexander was never in such a difficult position. How to get out from here? – because the logic of Diogenes was absolutely clear. If you want peace, relaxation, serenity, start now! Conquering the whole world is not a necessary condition for it... not even an unnecessary condition.

We are doing everything to disturb ourselves by our greed, our lust, our desire for more and more, our non-ending ambition to be at the top. Then what will you do at the top?

What did Edmund Hillary do on Everest? He just looked stupid and embarrassed, standing alone on that peak for no reason at all. He had risked his life, knowing well hundreds of people have died before in the same effort, and all knew perfectly well there is nothing to be found – it is just eternal snow.

But strange are the ways of man, strange is his craziness.

Just watch your desires, your longings, your ambitions and you will be able to see who is creating disturbances; otherwise peace is your nature...for nine months in the mother's womb you were in .eternal peace.

Peace is the stuff the whole existence is made of. It is only the stupidity of man that has disturbed everything around him, within him. And now he is looking for peace.

You are asking me, "What is peace for the rebellious man?"

Peace has only one taste, utterly delicious – the ultimate taste of existence itself. You just have to drop all that is disturbing, all that createsturmoil, all that creates tension, anxiety, anguish; you don't have to *achieve* peace – remember.

Peace is already there deep inside you.

Peace is what youare made of.

It is your very consciousness, your very being.

But such is the utter insanity of man that they even start making peace their ambition, they start desiring peace. And this is the greatest dilemma for every man who is in search of himself. He has to understand the contradiction.

You cannot desire peace, because desire is the disturbance.

What you desire does not matter. You may desire peace or you may desire power, you may desire money or you may desire meditation, it doesn't matter — because the nature of desire is always the same. It is a tension, its goal is in the future, and peace is in the present.

Peace is not a tension.

Peace is a non-tense, relaxed state oflet-go.

There is not even the ambition of peace. There is no desire, no ambition, because one has understood the simple arithmetic that every desire. creates conflict, every ambition takes you away from yourself.

The moment you drop all your desires and all your ambitions, suddenly you find you are sitting in peace within the temple of your being.

To describe our situation I will tell you a few stories.

No matter which girl he brings home, Tom finds disapproval from his mother. He asks his friend for advice. "Find a girl just like your mother, then she is bound to like her," advises his friend. So after much searching, Tom finally finds the girl. "Just like you said," he tells his friend. "She talks, dresses, and even looks like my mother, and just like you said, my mother likedher." "So," asks his friend, "what's happening?"

"Nothing," says Tom, "my father hates her!"

How to find peace? If you find a woman just like your mother, it is absolutely certain your father will hate her, and he will veto your marriage.

"Will my husband be permitted to stay with me during the delivery?" Mary asked the doctor in the maternity ward.

"Ah, yes," replied the doctor, "I also believe the father of the child should be present at its birth."

"I don't think that's a good idea," said Mary, "he and my husband don't get along too well together."

Life is such a ridiculous drama. It will be simply a miracle if you can find anywhere here something even resembling a faraway echo of peace.

Several mem bers of the Golden Age Club were being asked, "And why do you think God has permitted you to reach the age of ninety-five?"

Without hesitation one wealthy old lady said, "To test the patience of my relatives."

All old people are doing that everywhere in every family, just testing the peace of their relatives.

Hymie Goldberg looked very sad; his wife was sick, so he called the doctor. After examining Mrs. Goldberg, the doctor said to Hymie, "I am afraid it is bad news: your wife has only a few hours to live. I hope you understand there is nothing more to be done. Don't let yourself suffer."

"It is alright, doc," said Goldberg, "I have suffered for forty years, I can suffer a few more hours. It is not a big problem."

People who are living together are suffering together. People are in love with each other or in hate with each other.

The findings of psychologists are that the couples are nothing but intimate enemies. They both are sabotaging each other's life, pulling each other's leg, not allowing a single moment of peact. They are bringing a thousand and one questions, and each question finally becomes a fight.

The woman has a totally different kind of argumen-tation. She does not follow Aristotle; nobody knows whom she follows, what kind of logic she has, at what point she will suddenly start crying and weeping and tears will be coming. The man thinks, "My God, you would think I have been giving simply a rational answer, now what to do?"

He has been reading books and consulting in libraries about how to have a good married life, and he knows every argument. But one knows not what kind of logic this woman follows. Suddenly she starts shouting, throwing things – which is not at all logical. No book of logic suggests that you break plates and cups and saucers. But logic or not, seeing that the whole house is in an earthquake, it is better to accept defeat.

It is not a question of logical victory. Victory is always of the woman. You can have logic, she will have victory. This is a simple division.

So the poor husband has the logic. Every morning with his umbrella by his side, keeping his logic, he goes to the office... just wondering that perhaps poets are right, nobody understands the nature of woman. In fact there is nothing to understand. It is so simple: she does not know logicnothing else! So she creates a nuisance. If you cannot bring some sensible argument, the best way is to shout and create nuisance – as much as you can.

One of my prokssors, he was a professor of law and a very famous professor... I had nothing to do with his classes, but he once in a while used to invite me. He loved to argue and I used.to say to him, "Listen, I don't know law at all. I can argue because I know logic, but my logic will not be in the legal jargon. I don't know the legal jargon."

He said, "Still, you come. Without you I don't enjoy."

Once aweek he used to have a discussion class, and one day he said, "I shall tell you the secret of the great legal experts of the world. If you have the law in your favor, be very polite to the judge, be very polite to the court, just put your case in simple legal form. The law is in your favor – there is no need to do anything else.

"But if you are suspicious, you don't know whether the law is in your favor or not and you are sitting on the fence – the camel can sit at any side – then don't go alone. Let your secretary and your assistant carry big books of law – as big as possible. Make a great impression in the court, 'Here comes a great expert,' and quote so fast that even the judge cannot catch what you are talking about. Talking fast, and not giving any chance to anybody, and quoting... and don't be worried whether you are quoting from right books or wrong books, or whether you are just quoting from the page you are opening before you. Nothing matters! You simply make the impression of a great expert, on whose tongue all the books are just ready.

"You need not even look at the book to find the page. Quotepages, quote paragraphs; say 'on the seventeenth line, on the ninety-seventh page,' but don't give chances for anybody to see – you go on ahead. Before they can see the ninety-seventh page, you have moved so fast that they have to look at other pages. By the time they are looking at other pages, you have gone far ahead. Create such a cyclone of words that the judge is overwhelmed and forgets completely what is the case.

"And if you are certain that you are going to be

defeated, that the law is absolutely and clearly against you, don't be worried! Go with dignity, and shout as loudly as you can. And as you are shouting, and the whole court is. resounding with your shouts, go on hitting the table, throw the books. You are going to be defeated anyway, so create as much nuisance as possible, because sense is not in your favor – only nonsense can be in your favor!

"Make the judge afraid; throw books in such a way that they simply pass by the side of the judge. Don't be won;ied about contempt of the court or anything, don't listen. Victory is going to be yours – victory at all costs.

"Just watch the situation. If the law is favorable, then be logical. If the law is fifty-fifty, then create as much jargon and scholarship as possiblc. If the law is one hundred percent against you and defeat is absolutely certain, you have nothing to lose, then jump and shout and make the court almost a wrestling ground. Makb the judge feel that somehow the case has to be finished. No more hearings, no postponement, today it has to be fixed because this man can hit, he is throwing books this way and that way... at the most, contempt of court – who cares?

"In contempt of court you are taken out of the court – go shouting! And when you are brought in, come in shouting. Even if you are taken out by the armed guards three times in a single day for contempt of court, go out shouting, come in shouting. But make the judge feel that you are not the person to accept defeat. Murder may happen, but defeat is not possible. You may commit suicide then and there, but defeat can not be accepted."

The poets who have been saying that nobody

understands the nature of woman are just idiots, nothing else. Women don't know logic, but they know one thing – that the essential thing is not logic, the essential thing is victory.

So the man goes on insisting on logical argument, and the woman goes on insisting on being victorious. She does not care about your logical arguments. But a man who is trying to be logical and sensible is bound to be afraid of many things – what will the neighbors think, what if the children wake up? So he is trying to calm the woman down, but she will calm down only if victory is hers; otherwise she will put everything at stake. But the man has to think about his prestige in the neighborhood, about his job.

(*A woman who is present at the discourse starts laughing a very gutsy laughter.*)

Now listen to this woman...why does she laugh? She must have remembered similar incidences. Every woman knows more or less, but she must have seen a great drama!

A rebellious man first tries to understand the causes that are not allowing his natural flowering.

The basic thing has to be remembered: peace is not a goal, peace is your intrinsic nature. So whatever is preventing your natural growth, *that* has to be dropped. If it is anger, jealousy, greed, ambition, desiring, then they are nothing worth. You are wasting a tremendous opportunity of finding an inexhaustible treasure of blessings for stupid things which don't have any significance. Drop them! It is not renunciation, it is simply understanding. It is not becoming a monk or an ascetic. It is simply becoming a more conscious man.

The more conscious you are, the more peace will arise within the silences of your own heart.

It has always been there, there was just no bridge between you and it. And you were running all around, all over the world, searching for it everywhere – except in your own house.

CHAPTER 8

Existence is the
Only Temple

Beloved Osho,
Is renouncing the world and society part of a
rebellious spirit?

THE WHOLE PAST of man is full of those people who
have renounced the world and society. Renunciation
has almost become part of all religions, a foundational
principle.

The rebel is renouncing the past.

He is not going to repeat the past.

He is bringing something new into the world.

Those who have escaped from the world and society
are escapists. They really renounced responsibilities, but
without understanding that the moment you renounce
responsibilities you also renounce freedom.

These are the complexities of life: freedom and
responsibilities go together, or remain together. The
more you are a lover of freedom, the more you will be
ready to accept responsibility.

But outside the world, outside the society, there
is no possibility of any responsibility, and it has to be
remembered that all that we learn, we learn through
being responsible.

The past has destroyed the beauty of the word
responsibility. They have made it almost equivalent
to duty; it is not really so. A duty is something done

reluctantly, as part of your spiritual slavery. Duty to your elders, duty to your husband, duty to your children — they are not responsibilities. To understand the word responsibility is very significant. You have to break it in two: *response* and *ability*.

You can act in two ways — one is reaction, another is response.

Reaction comes out of your past conditionings; it is mechanical.

Response comes out of your presence, awareness, consciousness; it is non-mechanical.

The ability to respond is one of the greatest principles of growth. You are not following any order, any commandment; you are simply following your awareness. You are functioning like a mirror, reflecting the situation and responding to it — not out of your memory from past experiences of similar situations, not repeating your reactions, but acting fresh, new, in this very moment. Neither the situation is old, nor your response — both are new. This ability is one of the qualities of the rebel.

Renouncing the world, escaping to the forest and the mountains, you are simply escaping from a learning situation. In a cave in the Himalayas you won't have any responsibility. But remember, without responsibility you cannot grow, your consciousness will remain stuck. For growth it needs to face, to encounter, to accept the challenges of responsibilities.

Escapists are cowards, they are not rebels — although that's what has been thought up to now, that they are rebellious spirits. They are not, they are simply cowards. They could not cope with life. They knew their weaknesses, their frailties and they thought it was better to escape, because then you will never have to face your weakness, your frailty; you will never come to know any challenge. But without challenges how are you going to grow?

No, the rebel cannot renounce the world and the society, but he certainly renounces many other things. He renounces the so-called morality imposed upon him by the society; he renounces the so-called values imposed by the society; he renounces the knowledge given by the society. He does not renounce the society as such, but he renounces everything that the society has given to him. This is true renunciation.

The rebel lives in the society, fighting, struggling. To remain in the crowd and not to be obedient to the crowd, but to be obedient to one's own conscience, is a tremendous opportunity for growth. It makes you bring out your best; it gives you a dignity.

A rebel is a fighter, a warrior – but how can you be a warrior in a cave in the Himalayas? With whom are you going to fight?

The rebel remains in the society, but he is no longer part of the society. That is his renunciation, and that is his rebelliousness. He is not stubborn, he is not adamant, he is not an egoist; he just does not go on fighting blindly. If he finds something right, he obeys it, but he obeys his own feeling of rightness, not the commandment given by others. And if he sees that it is not right, he disobeys it – whatsoever the cost may be. He may accept a crucifixion, but he will not accept any spiritual slavery.

The situation of the rebel is tremendously exciting.

Each moment he is faced with problems because the society has a fixed mode, a fixed pattern, fixed ideals, and the rebel cannot go with those fixed ideals – he has to follow his own still small voice. If his heart is saying no, there is no way, no power, to force him to say yes. You can kill him, but you cannot destroy his rebellious spirit.

His renunciation is far greater than the renunciation of Gautam Buddha, Mahavira and millions of others. They simply renounced the society, escaped into the forest, into the mountains. It was an easier way, but very dangerous because it goes against your growth.

The rebel renounces the society and still remains in it, fighting moment to moment. In this way he not only grows, he also allows the society to learn that there are many things which are not right, but have been thought right. There are many things which are immoral but have been thought moral; there are many things which have been thought very wise, but they are really *otherwise*.

For example, all the societies of the world have praised virginity in women. It is a universally accepted ideal that the woman should remain virgin before marriage. In the middle ages.... Sometimes there is a small thin skin barrier in a woman's vagina and if the'woman makes love to somebody that small barrier prevents the sperm going to the egg.

The first thing the man is interested to know about is the small screen – whether it is intact or not. If it is not intact, then the girl is not a virgin. Sometimes riding on a horse or climbing a tree or in an accident that small screen can be broken, can have holes, although the girl is a virgin. In the middle ages it was impossible to get a husband for her, so there were doctors who used to make an artificial skin barrier and fix it so that the woman looked virgin, whether she was virgin or not. Stupidity has no limits.

In fact, virginity should not be a part of a truly understanding society. Virginity means the woman remains unaware of what she is going to face after marriage. A more compassionate society will allow boys and girls to know sex before they get married, so they know exactly what they are going for and whether they want to go for it or not. And a woman should be allowed to know as many people before marriage as possible — and the same applies to the man — because before deciding a right partner, the only way is to be experienced about many partners, different types of people.

But ignorance was propounded in the name of virginity, in the name of morality. Ignorance cannot be supported on any grounds. If in the world married people are so miserable, one of the major reasons is that they were not allowed to know many women, many men, before their marriage; otherwise they would have chosen, with more understanding, the right person who fits harmoniously with them.

Astrologers are consulted — as if the stars are worried about whom you get married to, as if stars are at all interested in you! Palmists are consulted, as if there are lines on your hand which can give indications for a right partner. Birth charts are consulted.... all these things are absolutely irrelevant. When you were born and when the woman was born has no relationship to the life that you are going to live.

But these were rationalizations. Man was trying to console himself that he has been trying every possible way to find the right partner.

There is only one way to find the right partner and that is to allow young boys and young girls to mix with as many partners as possible, so they can know the differences between women, the differences between men, and they can come to know with whom they are polar opposites, with whom they are just lukewarm, with whom they are passionately in a harmony. Except that, there is no way of finding the right partner.

A man of rebellious spirit will have to be aware about every ideal, howsoever ancient, and will respond according to his awareness and understanding – not according to the conditioning of the society. That is true renunciation.

Lao Tzu, an authentic rebel – more authentic than Gautam Buddha and Mahavira, because he remained in the world and fought in the world – lived according to his own light, struggling, not escaping. He became so wise that the emperor invited him to become his prime minister. Lao Tzu simply refused. He said, "It won't work because it is improbable that we can come to the same conclusions about things. You live according to the ideals your forefathers have given to you; I live according to my own conscience." But the emperor was insistent; he could not see that there was any problem.

The very first day in his court a thief was brought; he had been caught red-handed stealing from the richest man in the capital, and he confessed that he was stealing. Lao Tzu gave six months jail to both the richest man and to the thief. The richest man said, "What? I have been robbed, I am a victim and I am being punished? Are you mad or something? There is no precedent in history that a man whose money has been stolen should be punished and not the thief."

Lao Tzu said, "In fact, you should be given a longer term in jail than the thief – I am being much too compassionate – because you have gathered all the money of the city. Do you think money showers from the sky? Who has made these people so poor that they have to become thieves? You are responsible.

"And this will be my judgment in every case of stealing. Both persons should go to jail. Your crime is far deeper – his crime is nothing. He is poor and you are responsible for it. And if he was stealing a little bit of money from your treasures, it was not much of a crime. That money belongs to many of the poor people from whom you got it. You went on becoming richer and richer, and many more people went on becoming poorer and poorer."

The rich man thought, "This man seems to be crazy, utterly crazy." He said, "I want one chance to see the emperor." He was so rich that even the emperor used to borrow money from him. He told the emperor what had happened. He told him, "If you don't remove this man from the court you will be behind bars just like me – because from where have you got all your treasures? If I am a criminal, you are a far bigger criminal."

The emperor saw the situation, saw the logic of the situation. He told Lao Tzu, "Perhaps you were right that it will be difficult for us to come to the same conclusions. You are relieved from your services."

This man was a rebel; he lived in the society, he

struggled in the society. A rebellious mind can only think what he thought. He was not reacting; otherwise there were precedents and law books. He was not looking in the law books and the precedents; he was looking inside his own self, watching the situation – why are so many people poor? Who is responsible for it? Certainly those who have become too rich are the real criminals.

A rebel will renounce ideals, morals, religions, philosophies, rituals, superstitions of the society – but not the society itself. He is not a coward, he is a warrior. He has to fight his way and he has to make paths for other rebels to follow. And as far as the world is concerned...they are not the same thing, the *world* and the *society*.

In the past, the so-called religious people have renounced the society and the world, both. The rebel will fight against the society, renounce its ideals, and he will love the world, because the world, the existence, is our very source of life. To renounce it is to be anti-life. But all religions have been anti-life, life-negative.

The rebel should be life-affirmative. He will bring in all those values which make the world more beautiful, more lovable, which make the world more rich. It is our world – we are part of it, it is part of us – how can we renounce it? Where can we go to renounce it? The world is in the Himalayan cave as much as it is here in the marketplace.

The world has to be nourished because it is nourishing you. The world has to be respected because it is your very source of life. All the juice that flows in you, all the joys and celebrations that happen to you, come from existence itself. Rather than running away from it, you should dive deeper into it. You should send your roots to deeper sources of life and love and laughter. You should dance and celebrate.

Your celebration will bring you closer to existence, because existence is in constant celebration. Your joy, your blissfulness, your silence, will bring the silences of the stars and the sky; your peace with existence will open the doors of all the mysteries it contains. There is no other way to become enlightened.

The world has not to be condemned, it has to be respected. The rebel will honor existence, he will have immense reverence for life in whatsoever form it exists — for men, for women, for trees, for mountains, for stars. In whatever form life exists, the rebel will have a deep reverence. That will be his gratitude, that will be his prayer, that will be his religion, that will be his revolution.

To be a rebel is the beginning of a totally new kind of life, a totally new style of life. It is the beginning of a new humanity, of a new man.

I would like the whole world to be rebellious, because only in that rebelliousness we will blossom to our full potential, we will release our fragrances. We will not be repressed individuals, as man has remained for centuries...the most repressed animal. Even birds are far more free, far more natural, far more in tune with nature.

When the sun rises, it does not knock on every tree, "Wake up, the night is over." It does not go to every nest of birds, "Start singing, it is time for it." No, just as the sun rises, the flowers start opening on their own accord...not by an order from above, but from an intrinsic inevitability, from a joy, from a blissfulness, the birds start singing.

Once I used to be a professor in a Sanskrit college. Since there were no professors, quarters available immediately and I was alone, they made arrangements for me to live in the hostel with the students. It was a Sanskrit college, following the old traditional way: every morning every student had to wake up at four o'clock, had to take a cold shower and line up by five for a prayer.

I used to wake up on my own for many years, and in the darkness of the very early morning…and they were not even aware that I have come as a professor, because I had not started teaching yet. It was a mistake on the part of the government to send me to that college, because I had no qualifications to teach Sanskrit. It took six months for the government to correct their mistake. Bureaucracy moves slowest, just as light moves fastest. They are the two polar opposites – light and bureaucracy.

So I had no business there and the students had no idea that I was a professor…and instead of prayer they were all abusing God, abusing the principal, abusing the whole ritual – in a cold winter taking a shower, and it was absolutely compulsory.

I heard this situation. I said, "This is strange…instead of being in prayer, they are doing just the opposite. Perhaps these six years in this college will be enough for them; they will never pray in their whole life, they will never wake up early, never again. These six years, torture will be enough of an experience."

I told the principal, "It is not right to make prayer

compulsory. Prayer cannot be made compulsory; love cannot be made compulsory."

He said, "No, it is not a question of compulsion; even if I remove the order that it is compulsory, still they will pray."

I said, "You try."

He removed the order. Except me, nobody woke up at four o'clock. I went and knocked on the principal's door at four o'clock. He himself was asleep – he was always asleep. He never participated in the prayer himself. I said, "Now come on and see; not a single student out of five hundred has woken up, and not a single student is praying."

The birds sing not out of compulsion. This cuckoo is not singing because of any presidential order, because of emergency – it is simply rejoicing with the sun, with the trees.

Existence is a constant celebration.

The flowers have opened their petals not because of any order; it is not a duty, it is a response – a response to the sun, a respect, a prayer, a gratitude.

A rebel lives naturally, responds naturally, becomes at home and at ease with existence. He is an existential being.

That defines the rebel correctly – the existential being. Existence is his temple, existence is his holy scripture, existence is his whole philosophy. He is not an existentialist, he is existential; it is his experience. He is at ease with the trees, with the rivers, with the mountains. He does not renounce, he has no condemnation. He has only great honor in his heart, and gratitude. To me, this gratitude is the only prayer.

CHAPTER 9

The Rebel Is A Freedom
Unto Himself

Beloved Osho,
What is the difference between the old sage and the new rebel?

THE OLD SAGE was respectable, honored by the society in which he was born. He followed the rules and regulations of the people, he went through all the disciplines required for being a sage. He was part of the social structure – and even though there were thousands of superstitions, ugly institutions, exploitation, philosophies to console the poor and the oppressed, he affirmed them. He was never against any of the institutions the society has lived with for centuries. He was a follower of the old, of the ancient.

In a way he was a simple man, but deep down utterly repressed, because all social structures are repressive. He was not an individual in his own right, he was only a part of a certain society, or cultural group; that certain group worshiped him for the simple reason that he was fulfilling their ideals, their cherished goals. He was their representative.

For example, no Hindu sage has denied or condemned the ugly institution of the caste system. It is impossible even to conceive that a man of clarity and enlightenment will not see that the caste system is a special way of exploiting the poor and the oppressed. Man has behaved so inhumanly with these poor and oppressed; it has not happened anywhere else in the world, and this was happening in *this* country, which has created the greatest number of sages.

They talked beautifully about God, they sang beautifully about the other world, they lived a life prescribed by the society, absolutely according to the rules. The society was happy that they were so obedient, and they were happy because the society fulfilled their subtle egos – they were thought to be almost incarnations of God. So there was a mutual conspiracy between the so-called old sages and the social structures in which they were born.

The ancientmost scripture of the Hindus, the *Vedas*, prescribe rituals in which not only animals have to be sacrificed to satisfy the gods, but even human beings have to be sacrificed – to satisfy a god that nobody has ever seen. But no sage of those days raised his voice to say that this is absolutely ridiculous, utterly irreligious, unspiritual. They all went hand in hand with the society, supporting whatever the society's beliefs were by their writings and by their living.

Their only satisfaction was that they were worshiped – but to be worshiped is a tremendous nourishment for the ego. If the society wanted them to live naked, they lived naked; if the society wanted them to live in utter poverty, they lived in utter poverty. In a single word, the old sage was just the opposite of the new rebel. The old sage was the obedient, ego-fulfilling, repressed being. According to me, he was sick – spiritually sick.

The new rebel is not going to conform to the establishment and its interests. He is absolutely unconcerned about his respectability, reputation, honor, worship; he is not in need of any of these things. The people who are empty inside need all these decorations.

The new rebel is an enlightened being – he is fulfilled and deeply contented. He stands aloof and alone, with a clarity about everything. He will say it, whether it goes against the society, against the heritage, against the ancient tradition, against scriptures – it does not matter.

To the new rebel, truth is the only religion. For truth he is ready to sacrificed; for truth he is ready to be condemned; for truth he is willing to be crucified.

The new rebel is an individual, absolutely free from the chains of the crowd – although those chains were of gold. He is as free as a bird on the wing. He will not accept any cage, howsoever precious. Truth is his religion, freedom is his path. And to be himself, utterly himself, is his goal.

The old sage was a yea-sayer. The new rebel is a warrior – a warrior against all that is wrong and inhuman, against all that is stupid and unscientific. And there is so much stupidity proclaimed by all the prophets, all the saints, all the sages...so much superstitiousness deeply ingrained in every religion, in every tradition, in every society, that the new rebel has to fight his way out of all these entanglements.

His attainment of freedom from the old and the rotten, the irrational and the superstitious, is an absolute necessity to attain more consciousness. The more he fights against the wrong, the more he becomes right. The more he becomes right, the more he is at ease, at home.

The old sage was a pretender, a hypocrite.

The new rebel is an authentic human being.

He does not claim any specialness. He does not claim, "I am the only begotten son of God." He does not claim, "I am the only messenger of God." He does not claim that he is the reincarnation of God. He simply claims, and with pride and dignity, that he is a human being.

One of the most beautiful mystics, Chandidas, has a beautiful song. I have never come across any statement of more significance: *Sabar upar manus satya tahar upar nahin* – "The truth of man is above all, and beyond that there is nothing higher."

The new rebel declares the pride of man and the death of God – and the death of all the saviors and the prophets and the messengers, because they were trying to pretend to be higher and holier than ordinary human beings.

The new rebel is a declaration of being nobody, just an ordinary human being – simple, sincere, alert and aware – knowing oneself, and knowing that everybody else is as divine as he himself is. The new rebel is a declaration of a spiritual communism.

All those old sages were "superior beings," and they condemned humanity. They condemned human nature, they condemned human instincts. In their eyes, to be human was to be a sinner. For the new rebel, to be human – to be absolutely human, natural, and relaxed with your instincts, with your intelligence, with your intuitions – is the only spirituality there is. There is nothing higher than that.

The old sages destroyed the dignity of man. They destroyed the pride of being human, and they raised a hypothetical God to heights which are inconceivable.

They did these two things simultaneously – reducing man to the lowest possibilities, and raising a hypothetical God to the highest of heights.

The God was false, but it was a strategy, because then they could claim that they were closer to God, and far away from human beings; they could have a direct connection with God, either as God's only begotten son, as His only messenger, or as His incarnation in the world. The hypothesis of God was very useful because it helped the sage, the so-called saint, to raise himself and his ego to the highest peaks possible.

The new rebel has no hypothetical God.

He has a real human being.

His effort is to clarify, to unburden the human heart, to raise human consciousness to its highest peaks. The old sage had a God, ready-made. The new rebel is immensely creative. He is giving a challenge to the world: You have to create your own god within your own being, you have to *be* a god. And this god is not going to be against your humanity; on the contrary, it is going to be its absolute fulfillment, its blossoming, its flowering, its coming of age.

Man has suffered too much, he has been insulted too much. He has made himself into the ugliest creature in the world. He has accepted ideologies which proclaim him only as a sinner, and thousands of years of continual insistence have made wounds in his heart of deep guilt – guilt which does not allow him to live totally, which does not allow him to love intensely, which does not allow him to dance passionately, which prevents him and cripples him in every possible way.

The old sage was an agent of the establishment, of

the churches, of the priests, of the kings, of all those who had the power and wanted to retain the power – power to exploit, power to enslave. And the old sage did his job very well. His reward was only a phony ego.

The new rebel is not going to accept any guilt, because whatever is natural is right. It has to be refined, it has to be lived – not repressed, not forced into the unconscious, but brought into the conscious.

Everything that nature has given to man has to be used in such a way that life becomes an orchestra. Nothing is wrong – only things are not in their right places. And this is the work of centuries of saints and sages and prophets – the whole credit goes to these people. For their own ego fulfillment they played a role which is one of the ugliest phenomena in the history of man.

The new rebel is truly a sage. He lives with such totality – and so intensely, so coherently, so harmoniously – that wisdom arises as a by-product. His enlightenment is not a gift from any God; his enlightenment is a reward of his own effort. It is his own hidden treasure that he finds.

The more harmonious he becomes…. His religion will be harmoniousness – a natural, relaxed, conscious effort to create a music out of his life and to make it a dance and a celebration. The old sage was absolutely uncreative – he has not created anything that you can be proud of. The new rebel will be a creator; he will create poetry, he will create music, he will create sculpture, he will create songs. Fundamentally he will create a luminous life here on *this* earth, not after death, but *now.*

This rebellion has been needed for thousands of years. Now it is time: those who have courage should come out of their imprisonment and declare the death of God and the birth of a new man. As far as the old sages and saints of this religion and that religion, of this culture and that culture are concerned, the difference is not much, just superficial....

The mother gave her little girl some money to go to the movies, a treat she had never had before. When she came home, her mother asked, "How did you get on, dear?"

"Well, Mummy, it was a bit like Sunday school. At Sunday school they sing, 'Stand up, stand up for Jesus.' And in the movies they shout, 'For Christ's sake, sit down!'"

Not much difference...!

A Christian sage, a Hindu sage, a Jaina sage – not much difference. Their words may be different, their disciplines may be different – somebody is standing up, somebody is sitting down – but their basic approach is to support slavery, to condemn humanity, and to proclaim a God which is the greatest lie we have tolerated, for thousands of years.

There was a young priest who went to his first parish. The old priest arranged to be in back of the confessional, to see if the beginner did it right. The young man tried hard and asked afterwards, "I did not do too badly, did I, Father?"

"Well," said the old priest, "not too badly for the first time. But next time we can have a little less 'Whew!... Wow!...Gee!' and a lot more, 'Tut, tut, tut!'"

The young priest, listening to the sinners, was saying "Wow! Gosh!..."

All that is pleasure to man has been condemned. Pain, self-torture, has been supported. Misery, poverty, has been raised as a spiritual value – "Blessed are the poor, for they shall inherit the kingdom of God." It is strange that the people who are going to inherit the kingdom of God should be starving and dying in Ethiopia, should be starving in India, and the people who are going to be in hell are enjoying all the pleasures the world can offer. It is a very strange arrangement!

If the world is a school, then the poor should be given all the pleasures so they get a little bit ready; otherwise even in heaven they will feel too guilty to enjoy anything. They will bring their conditioning with them. But the society was happy that the poor be told that they would inherit the kingdom of God – there is no need of any revolution here, there is no need to revolt against the structures which are making them poor.

The old sage was anti-revolutionary. He was for those who were oppressing and sucking the blood of the people. The new rebel will not be an agent of the bloodsuckers, of the parasites. He will not say, "Blessed are the poor." He will not say, "Suffer your misery patiently, because after death you are going to inherit the kingdom of God."

There is no kingdom of God – that's why the rich people have never bothered about it, never even questioned it. They have allowed the priests to tell the poor that they will inherit the kingdom of God because the priests know there is no kingdom of God, that there is no God, and the rich know there is no God, and no kingdom of God. This is a fiction just to keep the poor poor, just to keep the slaves slaves, and to avoid revolution of any kind.

A young girl found herself alone at home one night, so she invited her boyfriend round. She took him into the front room, turned on the electric heater, turned out the light, poured him a drink, and sat him on the sofa. He stroked her hair, kissed her neck, then her lips. He crushed her to him, he pressed her back, he laid her down, he lay on top of her. Then he stopped.

"Go on, go on," she moaned. "Don't stop now, or I shall die."

"But dearest, I don't know what to do next. The movies always fade out at this point."

One needs some experience. The humble, the meek, the poor, the oppressed, they shall inherit the kingdom of God – and they don't have any experience of life and its pleasures, its joys, its songs, its dances. They will be simply standing there embarrassed, not knowing what to do.

But no rich man down through history has ever raised the question: "We make all the temples, all the churches; we pay all the priests, who are in millions around the world; we publish all the holy books and distribute them free; we donate to all kinds of charitable things – and we shall not inherit the kingdom of God? What nonsense are you talking? You are our servants; we pay you."

Nobody has ever objected. What could be the reason? The reason is that the priest and the rich people both know perfectly well that this is only a deception

– there is no God and no kingdom of God. This is a fiction to keep the poor people consoled.

The new rebel will bring rebellion in all dimensions of life.

He will transform this earth into a paradise.

He will create gods out of all human beings.

Every human being has the potential to be a god – because he can become enlightened, he can become pure consciousness. That's what a god is going to mean in the future. In the past, God was the creator. In the future, God will be the creation of human consciousness. It will be the highest peak of human celebration, of human luminosity, of human light.

The new rebel is the first man in favor of the birth of a great humanity, and to bring a great humanity onto the earth, all fictions have to be removed. They are obstructions, hindrances. They have done immense harm to man; they have left man with only wounds.

The new rebel will preach health and wholeness. Life will become our only temple.

Reverence for life will become our only religion.

CHAPTER 10

Ambition and Competition:
The Pillars of Society

Beloved Osho,
You have been talking on Your vision of the rebel
lately, and yet the atmosphere I feel around us at the
moment is particularly soft, loving, pliable.
To me, this feels like part of Your magic – that You are
showing us existentially that the rebel will be born
not out of the fumes of violence and unhappiness, but
from the fragrance of love and ecstasy.

THE REBELS WHO are born out of violence prove
finally to be antirebellious. The moment they are in
power their rebellion disappears. They become as ugly
as the predecessors they have replaced, because through
violence you cannot bring flowers of love. By sowing
the seeds of poison you cannot hope that the flowers
will be anything other than poison.

In the past the great misery has been that those
who were peaceful and loving, silent and ecstatic, were
not rebels. They could not conceive that a rebellion is
possible out of love, out of compassion, out of ecstasy.
Their perspective was not that clear about the future
possibilities. So people who were loving, people who
were peaceful, people who were religious, prayerful,
instead of becoming rebels simply became escapists;
that was their substitute for rebellion. They escaped to
the mountains, to the forests to live a peaceful, silent,
and blissful life.

In a way they were certainly selfish. They never thought about those whom they were renouncing; their compassion was not great enough and their peace was not strong enough – it was afraid of being disturbed. Their love was not great enough – it was afraid of being burned in the fumes of rebellion.

And on the other hand there were rebels, but they were not peaceful and they were not silent and they had no idea of any ecstasy. They had never known anything of meditation. They had no contact with the heart. Their rebellion was only a reaction of the mind. They were angry, enraged by all the exploitation, oppression, by all the inhumanity that the establishment had been doing to other human beings. Out of their anger, out of their violence, out of their rage, they rebelled. So those who were not capable of rebellion rebelled, and those who were really capable of rebellion escaped.

Those people who were full of violence and rage succeeded. But while they were going through the rebellion they were becoming more and more accustomed to violence, and when the power came into their hands, it came into the hands of violent people. Naturally they used that power for more violence. Now they had a great opportunity to destroy as many people as possible.

Sometimes their destruction became nonsensical. In the Soviet Union, Stalin killed at least one million people – but these one million people were not the rich people against whom he had rebelled, against whom the whole rebellion was planned. These were the poor people for whom the whole rebellion was a promise and a hope for a better future. And why were they killed? The reasons are absolutely idiotic.

Communism believes that there should be no private property, and when people are in power they become absolutely blind to human reality. For example, it is true that private property should not accumulate only in a few hands, and it should not make millions of people poor. To this extent communism is absolutely right. But to abolish private property completely is a very anti-psychological, unnatural idea.

It has to be understood...your private property gives you a certain individuality, a certain identity, a certain freedom. If all your private property is taken away and you are left absolutely naked, without any private property, you will be surprised to know that all your freedom is gone, all your individuality is gone, all your capacity to rebel is gone. In a certain way you have been murdered. Not only has your private property been taken away, you have also been finished.

Marx had no psychological insight; he was absolutely blind about the psychological and spiritual experiences of man. His whole approach was purely economic – but man is not just money. Man is much more. Man is not just what he possesses, he is much more. But what he possesses has a certain value as far as his individuality is concerned.

According to me, the right communism should be that accumulation of private property in a few hands should be stopped, so that everybody can have private property. Nobody is super-rich and nobody is super-poor. The rich disappear, the poor disappear, the middle class becomes the only class, and people have almost equal private properties. I am saying almost, because man should not be treated in mathematical terms.

There should be some looseness. Somebody may have a little more, somebody may have a little less; it does not matter, it does not hurt. Somebody may need... a doctor may need a private car, it is part of his profession, so to take away the doctor's private car is to take away something very essential to his profession.

So the millions of poor people who had not much – somebody has two cows, somebody has one horse, somebody has a few hens, somebody has a small piece of land.... But the blind mathematical and economic mind of the communists, which became even more blind when the. whole power was in their hands, started taking away everything from people – a small piece of land, which was not enough to provide food for the owners, but it was all that they had. It was their inheritance, their forefathers had it. Without it they suddenly found themselves utterly nude, as if their clothes had been taken away.

Their houses were not much, they were not palaces; they were living in the same house where their cows and their horses were living – they were stables more than houses. But even those were taken away. Everything became the property of the state. And these poor people, for whom the revolution was done, could not understand – what kind of revolution is this? They were thinking that they would become richer, that their poverty would be gone. But on the contrary, whatever they had – even that was gone. Now they were just beggars.

Capitalism had become concentrated in the hands of the state, so the people who were in power had, for the first time, double powers – the power of politics and all the power of economics. Before, it had been divided: the economic power was in the hands of the rich people and the political power was in the hands of the politicians – there was a little division. Now the power was absolutely totalitarian. All the power became concentrated in the hands of the people who were the rulers.

The poor people, who were uneducated, could not understand – what kind of equality is this? Are they making everybody poor, equally poor? Is this the equality for which the revolution was fought? And because they resisted giving their hens, their small pieces of land, their small houses, their horses or their cows... because they resisted, they were simply butchered.

Out of violence only more violence is born.

Those one million people were the lowest of the low. The revolution killed the poor people. It was a blind revolution, and it was bound to be because the rebels had no idea of compassion, no love for humanity, no experience of spirituality. They were not coming from that beautiful space; they were not fighting for a better humanity. They were simply only interested in destroying the establishment out of anger. In this anger there was jealousy, in this anger there was envy – all wrong things.

My effort is to bring a great synthesis between the rebel and the sannyasin. The sannyasin should not be escapist. He should grow his love, make his compassion strong enough, his ecstasy deep rooted, centered and mature. And out of this loving space, he should rebel.

His rebellion will be basically not interested in destroying the establishment, but interested in creating a new world. His focus is to create a new world, a new man, a new humanity with new values. To create the new he has to demolish the old – but not out of anger, just out of necessity.

And he has to understand that just to impose mental ideas on people is dangerous. You have to understand people's psychology and your rebellion has to be molded accordingly, not vice versa – not that the people have to be molded according to your idea of rebellion.

Man should never be used for any ideology.

All ideologies should be used for man.

Looking into man's psychology, it is true that vast distances between people create an ugly society.

Just a few days ago I was informed that in India there are only fifteen really rich people – in a country of nine hundred million people, only fifteen really rich people! So the whole wealth of nine hundred million people has been exploited; their labor, their whole life has been sucked by only fifteen families. This disparity is inhuman, because the producer is hungry and the parasite goes on collecting money which is useless to him. It is useful for those who are dying in hunger – and they are the producers.

These fifteen rich families don't work, don't produce; they are simply clever about how to suck blood. They have spread like an octopus around millions of people, and they are sucking their blood. In a thousand and one ways all the money goes silently, without any noise, into their treasuries.

You will be surprised to know that just the city of Bombay has half the money of the whole country. Strange… the whole country works – people are working in the fields, in the gardens, in the factories – but somehow there are strategies so that the money goes on moving towards Bombay. Half of the country's money in one city! This is intolerable – but one should not be angry about it. It is intolerable because it is inhuman and it destroys people's love, people's compassion, people's kindness. It creates all kinds of crime. Poverty is the mother of all crimes.

It is a very strange world. First you make people poor and force them to became criminals, and then you have courts and the police and the judges to punish them. First they are exploited, and then they are punished for being criminals.

The real criminals are those fifteen families who have exploited the whole country's wealth. But they will never be punished because they can purchase all your judges, they can purchase all your politicians. They already have all your politicians in their hands, because from where is the politician going to find millions of rupees for his election? Not from the poor people. And the people who are going to give him millions of rupees are not going to give it as charity. If they give one million, they will take out of that politician at least fifty million, not less than that. When he comes into power then all the licenses will go to the man who has brought him into power.

These politicians are all slaves to one capitalist party or to another capitalist family. They go on promising the poor a better future, and they know perfectly well that a better future is not going to come, because first they have to repay the money that has been given to them. They are themselves slaves.

This situation is ugly. The structure should certainly be changed. But it should be changed because you have a compassion, a love for all suffering human beings – not an anger, an envy, a jealousy against those few who have all the money, who have all the luxuries.

It is a question of focus: are you fighting for the poor? Or are you fighting because of your jealousy that you are not one of the fifteen families? Is it your jealousy, envy, anger, violence, that is prompting you to rebel against this structure? If that is the case, then when you are in power you will be more dangerous, because you will take as much revenge as you are capable of – with vengeance.

But if your revolution is because you have seen the suffering of humanity, you will create a structure which will give equal opportunity to everybody to grow. You will not impose the idea of equality, because equality simply does not exist; it is not psychological and it is not existential.

A Bertrand Russell is a Bertrand Russell, and if he has a little more comfortable life, he needs it; his contribution is so great that he should be provided with all the comforts possible.

An Albert Einstein is an Albert Einstein. He is not equal to anybody else in the world and nobody can claim to be equal to him. It will be simply stupid to force him to be equal – his work is different, his genius is different. In fact, he has not to be dragged down – he is not a shopkeeper and he is not a laborer. He should not be forced to be a shopkeeper, that will be a tremendous harm to the whole evolution of mankind, and he should not be forced to be a laborer, because nobody else can replace him.

Who is going to create the theory of relativity? Who is going to give us the tremendous power of atomic energy? It is unfortunate that the politicians have been using it in destroying man, but Albert Einstein is not responsible for it. The same energy could have been used for making man richer, healthier, for making the world more beautiful.

Men are not equal – that is my fundamental approach.

And secondly, it is my understanding that everybody should be allowed to have private property; just the distances should not be too big, they should be within human limits.

The whole country can be rich.

The state need not become the only owner of everything; that is the most dangerous thing which can happen to any country, because the state is already powerful. It has all the military, it has all the courts, it has all the police, it has all the laws, all the judges in its favor, and it wants all the finances of the country also to be in its power? Then the whole country is left absolutely nude, in the same state as beggars – "Now we don't have anything." And the state has become such a monster that you cannot even fight with it.

The state has gathered all the powers possible into its own hands. In Russia all the newspapers are published by the government. You cannot write an article criticizing any policy of the government because it will not be published anywhere. But if you write it, you will be behind bars. It will never be published, but *you* will go out of existence!

No book can be published, because only the

government has the right to publish anything. And you can see the results – in sixty years since the Russian revolution not a single Leo Tolstoy, or a Feodor Dostoyevski, or a Turgenev, or a Chekhov, or a Gorky… these five names are pre-revolution names. These five became world-famous novelists. If you have to choose ten great novels of the world, five will be Russian. These five names have to be included, there is no other way, because they have created the best masterpieces.

Where has that genius disappeared? In sixty years, not a single novel has come of that quality. It cannot come, because individuality has been completely destroyed. Now government bureaucrats decide what novels should be published and what should not be published, and these stupid bureaucrats don't have any sensibility. They are not poets, they are not novelists; they don't understand the subtle nuances of creativity. But they are now the decisive factors. So the best is not published, only the third rate – because only the third rate they can understand.

Just a few days ago one of my friends from Delhi informed me, "There is talk going on in the inner circles of the government that your books should first be censored, your tapes should first be censored, by the government. Only then can they be allowed to reach the masses."

I informed him, "Let them decide it, and they will have to face me in the Supreme Court!"

Who is the man – I would like to see his face – who is going to decide what is right in my book and what is wrong? I know all those ministers; I know most of the parliament members. They don't have the caliber or the intelligence. None of them have ever meditated; how can they decide whether what I am saying is right or wrong?

Tomorrow they may start asking scientists, "Before you publish your papers, government bureaucrats will see whether they are right or wrong." And the government bureaucrats have no idea of science, no idea of philosophy, no idea of poetry, no idea of music. If they had any idea of poetry and science and literature and philosophy, in the first place they would not have been bureaucrats! That is the ugliest thing in the world. To be a government bureaucrat means you have become part of an ugly machinery and you have lost your soul. You don't exist anymore as an independent thinker.

Rebellion out of love, rebellion out of creativity, rebellion out of meditativeness – that's my longing and that's my hope. And in that hope is the hope for the whole humanity.

We have to bring Gautam Buddhas to become rebellious.

Only in their hands will power be unable to corrupt; on the contrary, they will be able to purify power. And only in their hands is man's individuality safe, because they understand man's inner and outer existence and they will be able to help humanity.

They will not impose any equality, but they will give equal opportunity to everybody. Whatever one wants to become, he should be given equal opportunity. And then it is his potential, his talents, his genius...somebody will become a Bertrand Russell, somebody will become a Rabindranath Tagore, somebody will become a Picasso. And certainly the people who will be enriching life and existence should be given a more comfortable life, because they are serving in a way nobody else can serve. Their service is unique, and their uniqueness should be respected.

That does not mean that they are superior and higher, and you are smaller and lower. It simply means that we accept a fundamental fact about humanity: every man is just like himself, not like anybody else, and he will need certain private property, just as he needs his clothing.

In China, when Mao was in power, he even forced people to use only uniforms. These are the ways of destroying, in a very subtle way. Now the laborer is using the same uniform; the farmer is using the same, the philosopher is using the same, the mystic is using the same, the professor is using the same uniform. This is not right at all, because even your clothes show your individuality. You should have the freedom to choose your clothes; the government has not to decide.

You are not part of an army, so that you have to be in uniforms. You are independent individuals.

If equality is stretched to its logical end, then everybody should have the same haircut. And perhaps if some idiot gets into power... and idiots get into power more than intelligent people, because intelligent people don't want to go into the crowd and fight for power, it is not worth the whole struggle. But idiots have thick skin and hard skulls.

An idiot can even start thinking that people should have similar noses. A few people have beautiful faces, and a few people don't. This is not good for a society which is communist, which believes in equality. But now plastic surgery is possible... so make a model and let everybody go through plastic surgery. Every child when he is born can go through plastic surgery and you will see similar faces all around. Will that be a beautiful society? Is it right to harm humanity in such ugly ways?

I am against classes of poor people and rich people, but I am absolutely in favor of private property. The differences should not be too great, but differences should be allowed. And the state should not be the owner of all the property of the land. The politicians already have more power than they should have. To give them even more power, all power in their hands, is to commit suicide.

My rebel is a meditator.

He loves peace, he loves people, he loves their well-being, and he will do everything for their natural growth. He will not impose any ideology, he will simply help everybody to be himself.

Such a rebellion has never happened. But it is time – the right time. If it does not happen, then you can lose all hope for any future possibility of human existence as such. The old society has become so rotten that it is going to die. Before it dies, let us create seeds for a new man.

My insistence for a rebellion is to create those seeds, so when the old dies – it is bound to die, it has created its own death – the new can take its place. The new can be made alert and aware, so that it does not repeat the old pattern again. It is easier to repeat the old pattern, but once you are alert you never commit the same mistake again; it is only the stupid who go on committing the same mistakes again.

I have met a man who married eight times, and he was complaining to me, "I have wasted my whole life. I have searched for the right person, but I have not been able to find her. Every woman turns out to be the same."

I said, "You will be an example to others."

He said, "What do you mean?"

I said, "I simply mean that you are an ideal idiot. One woman was enough, at the most two... not to leave any chances, at the most three. But you went on and on, and every time it came to the same point. Eight or eighty, it will not make any difference, because *you* are the same. The differences in people are very superficial; they are like the differences in cars. Their bonnets are different, their headlights are different, but basically it is the same mechanism, the same engine, and if the driver remains the same he is going to fall into ditches again and again. Eight times is too much! You should have stopped driving long ago. You don't know how to drive."

He said, "Maybe, but nobody told me this."

I said, "You should have understood yourself. People are struggling in their own ditches; who is going to care about you?"

A rebellion which is religious, which is spiritual, which is not born out of the flames of violence but which is born out of the fragrance of love and compassion, out of meditation, alertness and awareness, is the only possibility for a transformation of this beautiful planet into a paradise.

Yes, what you are saying, exactly that I am trying to do. You are saying, "You have been talking on your vision of the rebel lately, and yet the atmosphere I feel around us at the moment is particularly soft, loving, pliable. To me, this feels like part of your magic – that you are showing us existentially that the rebel will be born not out of the fumes of violence and unhappiness, but from the fragrance of love and ecstasy."

Exactly that is what I am living for.

Exactly that is what I am preparing *you* for.

CHAPTER 11

Rebels Needed:
Only Individuals Should Apply

Beloved Osho,
What is a beautiful and enlightened chap like You doing
with a motley crew such as we?
Actually, I don't really want to know what You are
doing. Just, please, don't stop doing it.

EVERY CROWD IS a motley crowd, but no individual is motley. Every individual is an authentic consciousness. The moment he becomes a part of the crowd, he loses his consciousness; then he is dominated by the collective, mechanical mind.

You are asking me what I am doing? I am doing a simple thing – bringing out individuals from the motley crowds, giving them their individuality and dignity.

I don't want any crowds in the world. Whether they have gathered in the name of religions, or in the name of nationality, or in the name of race, it does not matter. The crowd as such is ugly, and the crowd has committed the greatest crimes in the world, because the crowd has no consciousness. It is a collective unconsciousness.

Consciousness makes one an individual – a solitary pine tree dancing in the wind, a solitary sunlit mountain peak in its utter glory and beauty, a solitary lion and his tremendously beautiful roar that goes on echoing for miles in the valleys.

The crowd is always of sheep, and all the efforts of the past have been to convert every individual into a cog in the wheel, into a dead part in a dead crowd. The more unconscious he is and the more his behavior is dominated by the collectivity, the less dangerous he is. In fact, he becomes almost harmless. He cannot destroy even his own slavery.

On the contrary, he starts glorifying his own slavery – his religion, his nation, his race, his color, These are his slaveries, but he starts glorifying them. As an individual he belongs to no crowd. Every child is born as an individual, but rarely a man dies as an individual.

My work is that you should meet your death with the same innocence, with the same integrity, with the same individuality as you have met your birth. Between your birth and your death your dance should remain a conscious, solitary reaching to the stars... alone, uncompromising – a rebellious spirit. Unless you have a rebellious spirit, you don't have a spirit at all. There are no other kinds of spirit available.

And you rest assured that I am not going to stop! That's my only joy – to make as many people free from their bondages, dark cells, their handcuffs, their chains, and to bring them into light, so they can also know the beauties of this planet, the beauty of this sky, the beauties of this existence. Other than that there is no God, and no God's temple.

In freedom you can enter the temple.

In a collectivity, in a crowd, you simply go on clinging to the corpses of the past. A man living according to the crowd has stopped living. He is simply following like a robot.

Perhaps robots are also a little bit more individual than the so-called individual in the crowd... because just now in Japan there are one hundred thousand robots – mechanical men – working in the factories. Suddenly, within these two months, a strange phenomenon is happening. The government is worried, the scientists are worried, and they have not been able to find any explanation. Up to now the robots have been working silently; nobody had ever thought that they will suddenly go into a rebellion. But ten people have been killed within two months.

A robot is working – and a robot works according to a computer, according to a pre-programmed plan; he cannot go in any way differently from the program that has been fed into it. But strangely enough, suddenly these ten robots stopped working, got hold of some man who was around, and just killed him. The figure of ten men being killed is from the government – it cannot be true. No government speaks the truth.

My own experience is that it is always good to multiply all the figures given by the government by at least ten. If they are saying ten persons have died, one hundred persons must have died, or more. They are trying to pacify the masses – "Don't be worried, we will find what went wrong." But they have no idea.

In fact, any act that is not programmed in the computer, the robot is not capable of doing – and these were not the programs. The robots showed some sign of freedom, they showed some sign of individuality, some indication of rebellion.

Computers cannot answer any new question. They can answer only questions for which information has already been given to them. Naturally – they don't have any intelligence, they have only a memory system, a filing system which records. Of course, they are perfect in their efficiency. No man can be that perfect; once in a while you forget.

And it is absolutely necessary, for life to go on, to forget most of the unnecessary things that are happening every day; otherwise your memory system will be too loaded. But the computer is a mechanism. You cannot load it too much, it has no life.

I have heard… a man was asking a computer, "Can you tell me where my father is?" He was just joking with the scientist who was working on that great computer, and the computer said, "Your father? He went fishing just three hours ago." The man laughed and said to the scientist, "You are creating a stupid computer. My father has been dead for three years." And he was shocked that the computer laughed – for which it was never programmed – and said, "Don't be gullible. It was not your father who died three years ago, it was only the husband of your mother. Your father has gone fishing three hours ago; you can go to the beach and you will meet him." Right now this is only a story, but looking at the actual facts happening in Japan, the story takes on a certain reality.

But man in the crowd has always behaved blindly. If you pull the same man out of the crowd and ask him, "What were you doing? Can you do it alone, on your own?" he will feel embarrassed. And you will be surprised to hear his answer: "On my own I cannot do such a stupid thing, but when I am in a crowd, something strange happens."

For twenty years I lived in a city which was proportionately divided, half and half, into Hindus and Mohammedans. They were equally powerful, and almost every year riots happened. I used to know a professor in the university where I was teaching. I could never have dreamed that this man could put fire to a Hindu temple; he was such a gentleman – nice, well-educated, well-cultured. When there was a riot between the Hindus and the Mohammedans I was watching, standing by the roadside. Mohammedans were burning a Hindu temple, Hindus were burning a Mohammedan mosque.

I saw this professor engaged in burning the Hindu temple. I pulled him out and I asked, "Professor Farid, what are you doing?"

He became very embarrassed. He said, "I'm sorry, I got lost in the crowd. Because everybody else was doing it, I forgot my own responsibility – everybody else was responsible. I felt for the first time a tremendous freedom from responsibility. Nobody could blame me. It was a mohammedan crowd, and I was just part of it."

On another occasion, a Mohammedan's watch shop was being looted. It was the most precious collection of watches. An old Hindu priest... the people who were taking away those watches and destroying the shop – they had killed the shop owner – were all Hindus.

An old priest I was acquainted with was standing on the steps, shouting very angrily at the people, "What are you doing? This is against our religion, against our morality, against our culture. This is not right."

I was seeing the whole scene from a bookstore, on a first story in a building just in front of the shop on the other side of the road. The greatest surprise was yet to come. When people had taken every valuable article from the shop, there was only an old grandfather clock – very big, very antique – left. Seeing that people were leaving, the old man took that clock on his shoulders. It was difficult for him to carry because it was too heavy. I could not believe my eyes! He had been preventing people, and this was the last item in the shop.

I had to come down from the bookstore and stop the priest. I asked him, "This is strange. The whole time you were shouting, 'This is against our morality! This is against our religion, don't do it!' And now you are taking the biggest clock in the shop."

He said, "I shouted enough, but nobody listened. And then finally the idea arose in me that I am simply shouting and wasting my time, and everybody else is getting something. So it is better to take this clock before somebody else gets it, because it was the only item left."

I asked, "But what happened to religion, morality, culture?"

He said this with an ashamed face – but he said it, "When nobody bothers about religion, culture and morality, why should I be the only victim? I am also part of the same crowd. I tried my best to convince them, but if nobody is going to follow the religious and the moral and the right way, then I am not going to be just a loser and look stupid standing there. Nobody even listened to me, nobody took any notice of me." He carried that clock away.

I have seen at least a dozen riots in that city, and I have asked individuals who have participated in arson, in murder, in rape, "Can you do it alone, on your own?" And they all, without any exception, said, "On our own we cannot do it. It was because so many people were doing it, and there was no responsibility left. We were not answerable, the crowd was answerable."

Man loses his small consciousness so easily into the collective ocean of unconsciousness. That is the cause of all wars, all riots, all crusades, all murders.

Individuals have committed very few crimes compared to the crowd. And the individuals who have committed crimes, their reasons are totally different – they are born with a criminal mind, they are born with a criminal chemistry, they need treatment. But the man who commits a crime because he is part of a crowd has nothing to be treated. All that is needed is that he should be taken out of the crowd. He should be cleaned; he should be cleaned from all bondages, from any kind of collectivity. He should be made an individual again – as he had come into the world.

The crowds must disappear from the world.

Only individuals should be left.

Then individuals can have meetings, individuals can have communions, individuals can have dialogue. Right now, being part of a crowd, they are not free, not even conscious to have a dialogue or a communion.

My work is to take individuals out from any crowd – Christian, Mohammedan, Hindu, Jew… any political crowd, any racial crowd, any national crowd – Indian, Chinese, Japanese. I am against the crowd and absolutely for the individual, because only the individual can save the world. Only the individual can be the *rebel* and the *new man,* the foundation for the future humanity.

The teacher is asking three boys in her class, "What

was your mother doing when you left for school this morning?"

"Doing the washing," says Tom.

"Cleaning the bedroom," says Dick.

"Getting ready to go out and shoot ducks," says Harry.

"What! What are you talking about, Harry?" asked the teacher.

"Well miss," says Harry, "my dad has left home, and she threw her knickers on the fire and said she was going back to the game."

People are imitators. People are not acting on their own grounds; they are reacting. The husband has left her; that becomes a reaction in her, a revenge – she is going back to the game. It is not an action out of consciousness, it is not an indication of individuality.

This is how the collective mind functions – always according to somebody else. Either for or against, it does not matter; either conformist or non-conformist, it does not matter. But it always is directed, motivated, dictated by others. Left to himself, he will find himself utterly lost – what to do?

I am teaching my people to be meditators; to be people who can enjoy aloneness, to be people who can respect themselves without belonging to any crowd, who are not going to sell their souls for any awards and honors and respectability and prestige that the society can give to them. Their honor and their prestige and their power is within their own being – in their freedom, in their silence, in their love, in their creative action – not in their reaction. What others do is not determinative of their life.

Their life springs from within themselves. It has its own roots in the earth and its own branches in the sky. It has its own longings to reach to the stars.

Only such a man has beauty, grace. Only such a man has fulfilled the desire of existence to give him birth, to give him an opportunity. Those who remain part of crowd have missed the train.

CHAPTER 12

Rebellion:
Now Or Never

Beloved Osho,
Since childhood I had a rebel inside of me, but I felt so powerless that I lived a life of submission rather than rebelliousness.
Now, listening to You, I see that this rebel within me could become the new man You envisage, but now I am no longer isolated, but one of many.
Can it be that we can all carry such a powerhouse within us that we could make it to the new world You envisage?

EVERYBODY IS BORN innocent, peaceful, loving... knowing nothing about the cutthroat competition in the world, knowing nothing about the nuclear weapons that are being prepared to welcome him, knowing nothing about the dirty politics that have been torturing humanity for millennia. But before his peace, his love, his trust can become a rebellious force, we start destroying all that is beautiful in him and replacing it with all that is ugly in us. That's what our parents have done to us, so we repeat the performance.

Generation after generation, the same disease goes on being transferred from one hand to another hand. With all the good intentions in the world the parents, the teachers, the leaders, the priests all go on forcing ideas of competition, comparison, ambition, preparing every child for the tough struggle that he is going to face in life – in other words, for violence, aggressiveness. They know that unless you are aggressive you will be left behind. You have to assert yourself, and assert forcibly, and you have to compete as if it were a question of life and death. All this is the framework of our educational system.

I used to come first in my class – not that I was studious, not that I attended the class regularly. I simply found that the courses we are teaching to students are not even worth two months' time, and we are wasting the whole year; so just for two months at the end I gave my total attention, and the remaining time I was enjoying everything else except school.

The teachers were amazed! And when I used to come home after the results and I would tell my father that I had come first, he always said, "That means your class consists of fools."

I said, "This is strange. When other people come first their parents feel happy and you, it seems, feel sorry that I am studying with fools. That's why I have come first; otherwise there is no hope for me."

But he never encouraged me, "You have done a good job, you should be rewarded" – he never rewarded me. His only expression always, consistently was, "It is strange how you can always find a class of fools, so naturally you come first." But it is very rare. Parents give every incentive, "Be first and you will be rewarded." Be first – that is bringing honor to the parents, to the family.

Everybody is teaching you to be ahead of others, whatever the cost. Sooner or later, the children become feverish, they start running faster. Even if they have to hurt somebody to get ahead, they will do it. Violence is bound to be a part of a competitive society.

In a competitive society you don't have any friends. Everybody pretends to be friendly, but everybody is your enemy because everybody is fighting to climb on the same ladder. Everybody is your enemy because he can succeed and force you to be a failure. And soon people start learning the art of how to pull on others' legs, how to use wrong means, because those wrong means give you a shortcut.

I used to know a student...I was a teacher in the university. On the examination days no teacher was ready to be in any hall where that student was given a place, because that student was almost murderous; at any moment he could murder somebody. What he used to do was this: he would come with a knife into the examination hall, and he would put his knife on the desk so everybody could see it there, and no professor would come close. He would bring notes with him and he would just manage to come first.

No professor wanted to be the observer in the examination hall where that student was. My vice-chancellor asked me.

I said, "There is no problem."

He said, "But nobody is ready..."

I said, "They don't understand."

I asked one of my friends – he was a Sikh. I asked him, "You give me your *kripan*." It was a big, special kind of sword, far more dangerous than any other sword. Just one hit and the head is off!

He said, "What are you going to do with the sword?"

I said, "I am trying to teach him to be a Sikh."

He said, "That is good. *Vah guruji ki fatah. Vah guruji ka khalsa.*"

That is the mantra of the Sikhs, "This is the way the victory of the master happens. This is the way the victory of the master's followers happens."

He gave me his kripan, and I went into the room. That boy was sitting with his small knife on the desk. I went near to his desk, and just by the side of his knife I forced my kripan into the wood. He looked at me and I said, "Throw away all the copies that you have brought with you. Just look at my kripan."

And I took away his knife. He said, "What are you doing?"

I said, "If you speak another word, just one hit of the kripan – you will lose your head."

He said, "You seem to be insane. I have not done anything wrong and you are ready to kill me!"

I said, "It is not a question of right or wrong. It is a question of who has a bigger knife – I have a bigger one! And I have all the powers in this examination hall to throw you out." And I threw his knife out of the hall.

I said, "If you don't throwaway all the copies that you have brought with you, your head will go from the same window." He gave me all his copies, and I threw them from the same window.

The vice-chancellor was watching from his room. "What is happening? – things are coming out. First the knife came, then a few books came." He came running – "It seems there is some trouble."

I said, "You don't be worried. Only one thing more…if this boy is not going to behave, you will see one more thing coming out of the window."

He said, "What?"

I said, "His head!"

He took me out and he said, "I am sorry that I asked you to be the examiner here. Just forgive me, don't do such a thing!"

I said, "There is no other way to teach that idiot a lesson. Because all the professors you have been sending here were so afraid of his knife, now nobody is ready to come. What can he do? – at the most he can kill you, so I have brought a bigger kripan."

But this is what the society makes everybody learn sooner or later: you have to be more aggressive, otherwise you will be a failure. You have to fight your way, because everybody is trying to reach the same ambition.

The vice-chancellor told me, "You are relieved. Never again are you required to be the examiner."

I said, "That is really great. That is what I wanted. It is unnecessary, because I don't want to harass anybody. Life will harass all of them – why should I add more harassment to their lives? But I cannot allow anybody to harass me, either. It is very good of you to have relieved me forever."

He looked at me. He said, "Yes, I can come with the kripan into your room too."

I said, "It doesn't matter whose head the kripan cuts. The kripan makes no difference."

He said, "What do you mean?"

I said, "I am simply saying that that boy is going to be first every year because you are all chickens, unnecessarily afraid. He can simply show you the knife and that's all."

But this whole society is violent, and you have to be more violent if you want to be ambitious.

I want the non-ambitious, the non-competitive man, a man who has no will for power, to be the rebel. Every child can become such a rebel; all that he needs is not to be distracted from his innocence.

Your feeling is right that you have a rebel inside you. Everybody has a rebel – but the society is too powerful. It makes you cowardly, it makes you cunning. It does not make you your authentic self. It does not want anybody to be his authentic self, because then there will be rebels all over.

But remember that before becoming a rebel you have to fulfill a few conditions. I don't want old-fashioned rebels. My rebel is also going to be a totally fresh and new idea, a new realization.

Unless you have compassion enough, love enough, silences of the heart, deep inner meditations bringing you more light, more awareness, you have not fulfilled my conditions. Only with these conditions do I want you to be a rebel. Then you cannot do anything wrong. Then whatever you do is right.

Out of love, everything is right.

Love is the magic that transforms everything into right.

I want enlightened rebels. It is possible, because enlightenment has been possible, rebels have been there. All that we need is a synthesis bringing them together – rebelliousness and enlightenment, a Gautam Buddha with the rebelliousness of a Lenin. It will be the most beautiful phenomenon.

One friend from Japan sent me a statue of Gautam Buddha. It was a I rare statue, l have never seen such a thing. In one of the hands of the statue there was a small earthen lamp with a flame. You had to put purified butter – ghee – inside the earthen lamp as fuel, so that the flame goes on burning. My friend said, "This is a condition – I had been given this statue with the same condition – that the flame should be burning twenty-four hours a day without a break." In the other hand the statue had a naked sword. This is possible only in Japan, because Japan has made even swordsmanship a meditative art and archery a meditative art. Meditation is basic.

In India we cannot conceive of Gautam Buddha having a sword. But the beauty of the statue was that half of his face was so peaceful, where the light of the small flame was falling – so calm and quiet, utter serenity, and on the other side his face was like the sword, so sharp that it could be only that of a great warrior. The artist who created it must have done tremendous work. In the same face he has shown a great synthesis – a sword in the hands of peace.

This is my idea of the rebellion, of the rebel. It should come out of your love for humanity, not out of anger against the past but from a creative compassion for the future. You are not just to destroy the old. Your ideal, your end, is to create the new, and because the new cannot be created without demolishing the old, you demolish it. But there is no anger in it. It is a simple process. You demolish an old building – there is no question of anger. You clean the place and make a new building in its place.

A sannyasin has to be both: the peace, the silence, the light, the qualities of his inner being, and a rebel against all injustice, against all inhumanity. But for a creative purpose...to materialize a dream of an authentic human society which will be able to give equal opportunity to all, freedom to all, education which is nonviolent, education which is not only informative but also transformative, an education that will make you more of an individual and bring the best in you to its flowering.

You are sitting with people who all have such dreams. And the people in the outside world also had once – when they were small children – the same qualities, which have been forced down, repressed. Their inhibitions can be removed.

My sannyasins have to become burning torches moving around in the world, to share their fire with anyone who is ready.

And you will be surprised, there are no people who have never dreamt of a beautiful future and who have never been in a state of innocence, who have never tasted something of peace, something of love, something of beauty. But all this has been destroyed, distorted, contaminated, poisoned by an ugly society. Its only power in its ancientness.

But now that very power, that ancientness, is going to prove its greatest weakness. It just needs a little push. It is a dead society already. It has prepared its grave with its own hands and it is standing just on the corner of the grave. You just have to push and you will suddenly find Ronald Reagan lying in his grave. And with

Ronald Reagan goes the whole world of which he is the representative.

We have to start from scratch. Again Adam and Eve, again the garden of Eden...again the very beginning.

CHAPTER 13

Your Light is the Only Right Light – for You

Beloved Osho,
Are Your sannyasins all rebels? Is it true that a rebel is
born and not made, or are we born rebels but tamed
and conditioned by our societies?

ONE WHO IS not a rebel will not come close to me.
The very fact that he comes close to me, becomes an
initiate, is proof enough that he is a rebel.

All my sannyasins are rebels.

No other kind of people can be my sannyasins.

Those who are not rebels are going to be against me,
because whatever I am saying goes against the whole past
of mankind – all its traditions, cultures, civilizations,
religions.

Unless one is ready to disconnect himself from the
past and the shadows of the dead, he cannot become a
sannyasin, because my sannyas has no past. It has only
future.

It has no connections with the past, it is discontinuous
with all that is old and dead. Its only concern is for the
future growth of your being, your consciousness, your
whole individuality.

That's exactly the meaning of being a rebel: to live
according to your own light, howsoever small, and
find your way in the unknown future. Give all the
opportunities, accept all the challenges of the unknown
fearlessly, as if you are the first people on the earth.

The past is a burden, and if you are attached to the past you cannot move a single inch. You are burdened with a mountain, your potentiality is going to be crushed. That has been happening for centuries – people are living so burdened, so conditioned, that there is no possibility for them to be themselves. They are Christians, they are Hindus, they are Mohammedans, but they are not themselves.

My sannyasin does not belong to any ideology, to any philosophy, to any theology. He is pure of all that is rotten, he is pure of all that has passed. His eyes are fixed on the future. He is seeking and searching his own growth, without any fear of the crowd, the masses – which don't have any individuality of their own. They are sheep, a crowd of sheep.

My sannyasin is a rebel. He comes out of the crowd, stands alone like a lion, finds himself – his path, his dignity, his freedom.

You are also asking, "Is it true that a rebel is born, not made, or are we born rebels but tamed and conditioned by our societies?"

A rebel is born, not made. In fact, nothing that is significant in human life is manufactured, is made. It is all intrinsic, inborn – you bring it with your life into the world. But you are born in a society, in a crowd, and that becomes a calamity, because the people you are born among and the people you will be growing with have no respect for individuals, particularly for children.

They think that their children are their possessions, and their whole effort is to fulfill their own incomplete ambitions through their children. They are frustrated. They have been running after shadows, they have not been able to attain any fulfillment. Now their only desire is that what they have not been able to do their children will do. At least there will be some satisfaction because their children are part of them, their blood. Through their children they will live.

This idea of living through children is immensely dangerous. It means you will not allow the child to be himself – he has to be somebody that you want him to be. And you cannot have any idea...there is no way to find out what the child was going to be if he were given freedom and support just to be himself. You help the child but you help the child with a condition – told or untold – that "You have to be the fulfillment of our desires, the representative of our longings, the completion of our ambitions."

That's why nobody is what he was meant by nature to be; he is somebody else. And you cannot be happy with being somebody other than yourself. You can pretend, but you are only playing a role imposed upon you; you are not being authentic and original. If you are a Catholic, can you think that if you had been left alone, without any imposition by your parents and the society to be a Catholic, you would have been a Catholic? Then there is the whole sky open to you, to choose. If you choose according to your own inclination, according to your own intuition...which is very strong in children but slowly, slowly becomes weaker. The voices of the parents and the teachers and the society and the priest become louder and louder. Now if you want to find out what is *your* voice, you will have to pass through a crowd of noises.

It is a tremendously beautiful experiment for

meditators just to watch inside – whose voice is this? Sometimes it is your father, sometimes it is your mother, sometimes it is your grandfather, sometimes it is your teacher. And those voices are different. Just one thing you will not be able to find easily – your own voice. It has been suppressed always. You have been told to listen to your elders, to listen to the priest, to listen to the teachers. You have never been told to listen to your own heart.

You are carrying a still, small voice of your own, unheard, and in the crowd of voices that have been imposed upon you, it is almost impossible to find it. First you will have to get rid of all those noises, attain a certain quality of silence, peace, serenity. Only then will it come, as a surprise; that you also have your own voice. It was always there like an undercurrent.

Unless you have found your natural inclination, your life is going to be a long, long tragedy, from the cradle to the grave. The only people who have been blissful in the world are the people who have lived according to their own intuitions, and have rebelled against any effort by others to impose their ideas. Howsoever valuable those ideas may be, they are useless because they are not yours. The only significant idea is that which arises in you, grows in you, blossoms in you.

Everybody is born a rebel because everybody is born to be an individual in his own right. Everybody is born not to be a part in a drama but to live an authentic life, not to be a mask but to be his original face. But no society till now has allowed people to be themselves. Once in a while a person has escaped – a Gautam Buddha, a Zarathustra, a Chuang Tzu, a Kabir. These people suffered all the condemnation of the society, but they found the joy of being themselves. All the condemnation of the society was nothing in comparison to the joy that they found. They suffered laughingly....

When Al-Hillaj Mansoor was killed by the orthodox, the traditionalists, because he was saying things which were rebellious, almost a million people gathered to see this ugliest possible murder. The crucifixion of Jesus seems far more cultured, because Al-Hillaj Mansoor was cut into pieces. His legs were cut off, his hands were cut off, his eyes were taken out – piece by piece. This was a torture perhaps no other man has ever gone through, but there was a smile on his face. Under all this inhumanity, barbarousness....

One of the men who was cutting off his hands, could not resist his temptation to ask, "Why are you smiling? Even I am feeling immensely miserable and sad and guilty. But this is my duty, this is my job. Why are *you* smiling?" And what Mansoor said is something to be remembered. He said, "I am smiling because you are killing somebody else. You are not killing me – that is beyond your capacity. I know my self, which no fire can burn and no sword can kill. You can cut the body... I am just smiling at the foolishness of you, and the emperor who has ordered this stupid act."

Everybody is a born rebel, that's why it is so easy to transform anybody who is still alive. Just a little understanding, a little encouragement, and he can be helped to drop his whole past and be reborn. Everybody can become a rebel.

A female gorilla was turning down all her male suitors. The zoo desperately needed some baby gorillas, and the zookeeper was at a loss as to what to do about it. While driving home that evening, the keeper notices a hairy Italian man walking about without a shirt on, and pulls his car up alongside him. "Hey," he calls, "I will pay you five hundred dollars if you will come to the zoo tomorrow morning, and make love to our female gorilla."

"Vai funculo buddy," says the offended Italian, "you have some nerve!" And he storms off. At home that night he relates the incident to his wife, who throws up her hands and cries, "Mamma mia! We are so poor, we need-a the money. So tomorrow you-a go and make love-a to this gorilla, or don't-a come home to-a Mamma."

The next morning at the zoo, the Italian is about to climb into the gorilla's cage when he turns to the zoo keeper and says, "Look, I will make-a love to this-a gorilla for three conditions. First-a, I don't-a have to kiss it. Second-a, I do it once. And third-a, when the kids are born you raise them as-a Catholics."

CHAPTER 14

Total Freedom –
Nothing Less!

Beloved Osho,
Is the path of the rebel the middle path, or the path of extremes?
I have heard You speak for and against both, and also say that there is no path.
What guides the rebel?

THE REBEL HAS no path to follow; those who follow any path are not rebels. The very spirit of rebellion needs no guidance. It is a light unto itself.

The people who cannot rebel ask for guidance, want to be followers. Their psychology is that to be a follower relieves them of all responsibility; the guide, the master, the leader, the messiah becomes responsible for everything. All that is needed of the follower is just to have faith. And just to have faith is another name of spiritual slavery.

The rebel is in a state of tremendous love with freedom – total freedom, nothing less than that. Hence he has no savior, no god's messenger, no messiah, no guide; he simply moves according to his own nature. He does not follow anybody, he does not imitate anybody. Certainly he has chosen the most dangerous way of life, full of responsibility, but of tremendous joy and freedom.

He falls many times, he commits mistakes, but he is never repentant of anything, because he learns a deep secret of life: by committing mistakes you become wise. There is no other way of becoming wise.

By going astray you become acquainted more dearly with what is right and what is wrong, because whatever gives you misery, suffering, makes your life a darkness without end, without any dawn; it means you have gone astray. Find out – and come again to the state of being where you are peaceful, silent, serene, and a fountain of blissfulness, and you are again on the right path. There is no other criterion than that.

Being blissful is to be right.

Being miserable is to be wrong.

The pilgrimage of the rebel is full of surprises. He has no map, no guide, so every moment he is coming to a new space, to a new experience – to his *own* experience, to his *own* truth, to his *own* bliss, to his *own* love.

Those who follow never know the beauty of experiencing things firsthand. They have always been using secondhand knowledge, and pretending to be wise. People are certainly very strange. They do not like to use secondhand shoes; even on their feet they will not put secondhand shoes. But what garbage they are carrying in their heads... just second hand shoes! All that they know is borrowed, imitated, learned – not by experience, but only by memory. Their knowledge consists of memorizing.

The rebel has no path as such.

He walks and makes his path while walking.

The rebel is almost like a bird flying in the sky; what path does he follow? There are no highways in the sky, there are no footprints of ancient birds, great birds, Gautam Buddhas. No bird leaves any footprints in the sky; hence the sky is always open. You fly and make your path.

Find the direction that gives you joy. Move towards the star that rings bells in your heart. You are to be the decisive factor, nobody else!

That's why I have spoken about the middle way many times when I was contradicting the people who follow the extreme, because the extreme can never be whole. It is only one polarity. In certain contexts I have contradicted them, saying that to be on one polarity is to miss the other polarity, is to live only half of life. You will always remain missing something tremendously valuable, and you will never know what it is. In that context I have talked about the middle way.

The man who walks the middle way, the golden mean – exactly in the middle – has both the extremes, like two wings reaching to the farthest corners. He comprehends the whole polarity in his being. He stands in the middle, but his wings reach to both the extremes simultaneously. He lives a life of wholeness.

But in another context, I have spoken *against* the middle way – because life is not so simple to understand. It is the most complex phenomenon in the world. It has to be, because it is the most evolved state of consciousness in the whole existence.

Its basic complexity is that you can never speak about it in its totality; you can only speak about one aspect. And when you are speaking about one aspect you are automatically denying other aspects, or at least ignoring them, and life is a combination of all contradictions. So when you are talking about one aspect, the contradictory aspect of it – which is also part of life, as much as the aspect you are speaking about — has to be denied, negated.

To understand me means to understand everything in a certain context. Never take it out of context; otherwise you will be simply bewildered, confused. Sometimes I have spoken of the middle way because, as I have told you, it comprehends the whole of life; its beauty is its totality. Sometimes I have spoken in favor of the extremes, because the extreme has its own beauty.

The life of the man who walks in the middle is always lukewarm. He is very cautious. He takes every step very calculatedly, afraid that he may move to the extreme.

The man who follows the middle way cannot live passionately; he cannot burn his torch of life from both ends, simultaneously. For that, one has to learn life at the extreme points. The extreme point knows intensity, but it does not know wholeness. So when I was talking about intensity, I have emphasized the extremes. But these were all spoken in a certain context.

I have also said that there is no path. With the idea of a path, we always conceive of highways, superhighways, which are already there — you have just to walk on them. That's why I have been denying that there is any path.

In the world of reality, you have to create the path while walking on it. As you walk you create, by and by, a footpath; otherwise you are entering into an unknown territory with no boundaries, no pathways, no milestones. Your walking is creating a path, certainly, but you cannot follow it; you have already walked on it — that's how it has been created.

And remember, *your* path is not going to be anybody

else's path, because each individual is so unique that if he follows somebody else's path he loses his own identity, he loses his own individuality, and that is the most beautiful experience in existence.

Losing yourself, what are you going to gain? You will become simply a hypocrite. That's why all so-called religious people are the worst hypocrites in the world; they are following either Jesus Christ or Gautam Buddha or Mahavira.

These people are not only hypocrites; these people are also cowards. They are not taking their own life in their own hands, they are not being respectful of their own dignity, they are not trying to figure out, who am I? They are simply trying to imitate somebody else. They can become good actors but they can never become themselves. And your acting – howsoever beautiful, howsoever correct – will always remain something superficial, just a layer of dust on you. Any situation can scratch it, and your reality will come out.

You cannot lose your uniqueness.

That is your very being.

And particularly the rebel...his very foundation, his very spirituality, his whole being is an assertion of his own uniqueness. It does not mean that he is asserting his ego, because he respects your uniqueness too.

People are neither equal, nor are they unequal. Those philosophies are absolutely unpsychological, unfounded in scientific truth. The very idea of equality is absolutely baseless. How can you conceive unique human beings to be equal?

Yes, they should be given equal opportunity – but for what? For a very strange reason. They should be given equal opportunity to grow to be themselves. In other words, they should be given equal opportunity to be unequal, to be unique. And the variety of different flowers, of different colors, of different flavors, makes the world rich.

All the religions have tried to make the world poorer and poorer. Just think, today the population of the world is coming close to – perhaps by the end of this month it will be – five billion. Just think, five billion people like Mahavira, walking naked all over the earth. They will not even find food. Who is going to give to them? where are they going to beg? because wherever they turn they will find another Mahavira, standing naked and hungry, asking for food.

It is good that people are not so stupid, that they have not followed all these people all the way. They said goodbye to them and said, "We will worship you, we will make temples for you, but forgive us, we cannot come that far. That is only for special people" – only for twenty-four people in the whole creation, out of which historians think twenty-one are absolutely bogus, they never happened. Only three are historical figures. But at that time the idea and the number of twenty-four had become certainly very strong.

Sometimes numbers also have their days. In America, number thirteen is thought to be very dangerous. Now, it is a poor number like any other number; in the whole world nobody thinks anything about number thirteen. But in America, hotels simply don't make the thirteenth floor; they don't number it. There it is – after twelve comes the fourteenth! The thirteenth simply does not come, because nobody wants to stay on the thirteenth floor. The municipal corporations cannot put the number thirteen on any house; number thirteen is simply missing in every city. After twelve comes fourteen, because nobody is willing to have number thirteen, it is evil.

In the days of Mahavira, the number twenty-four became a very spiritual number. These things happen like fashion. You cannot give any very reasonable evidences for why they happen.

Jainas declared they have twenty-four *tirthankaras*. Number twenty-four became important because the day has twenty-four hours, and the whole creation is conceived like a day – half will be dark night, and half will be full of light.

In one creation there will be twenty-four tirthankaras… just like old grandfather clocks with a bell that rings every hour. Still on city towers and in the universities those kind of clocks exist.

Nobody wants those clocks in the home, because the whole night you cannot sleep. The clock has no consideration whether you are asleep or awake; it simply goes on mechanically.

The mechanics of existence, according to Jainism, is that each hour of existence – that means millions and millions of years – will be preceded by one tirthankaras and succeeded by another. That's why there are twenty-four tirthankaras. Only three, or at the most four, the fourth is a little suspicious… but twenty are certainly a creation of imagination to complete the number twenty-four.

Gautam Buddha…his followers certainly must have felt, "We are very poor, we have only one buddha and these people have twenty-four tirthankaras, all awakened, all enlightened. Our religion is very poor, something has to be done." It is a clear-cut competition in the marketplace! They could not say that there have been twenty-three buddhas before, because there was no indication in their history, no temple dedicated to any other buddha, no scripture describing any other buddha. It was very difficult for them, so they found a new way.

They created a story that Gautam Buddha himself had been born twenty-three times before. Whatever he had said before, he was going to say it completely refined, well-systematized, on the twenty-fourth time, when he would be coming for the last time to the world – and that's why no scriptures exist. But they managed the number twenty-four.

Up to that time Hindus had only ten *avataras*, ten incarnations of God. Suddenly they felt...up to Mahavira's time all Hindu scriptures describe only ten incarnations of God. But suddenly they saw that they looked poor in the marketplace, if anybody asked – just ten? Jainas have twenty-four, Buddhas have twenty-four, twenty-four is the universal law, because these were the only three religions in India at that time.

Hindus were at a great loss, what to do? – because all their old scriptures say that there are only ten incarnations. They were in a more difficult situation than Buddhists. At least Buddhists had no scriptures, so they managed a beautiful story: nothing was recorded because in his last incarnation Buddha would say the most refined version. Twenty-three times he has rehearsed, the twenty-fourth time he will come with absolute perfection. That time it will be recorded, the statues will be made, temples will be made. At least nothing was contrary to their imagination; they could manage, in the vacuum, to fill the gaps with imaginary buddhas.

But Hindus were in more difficulty. All their scriptures, without any exception, were talking only about ten. But they started writing new scriptures, without bothering that this was creating a tremendous contradiction. All the scriptures created by the Hindus after Buddha and Mahavira have twenty-four reincarnations of God. The number has to be equal!

These religions have not been teachers of truth.

These religions have been just enslavers of humanity.

They were trying to bring as many people into their herd as they could, because numbers bring power. And the cowards were ready to follow the herd, the crowd, because the cowards were feeling alone, afraid. This vast universe, and you are alone…nobody, not even a companion – utter silence of the skies, nobody to show you the path, nobody to give you guidance.

The rebel is the real spiritual being. He does not belong to any herd, he does not belong to any system, he does not belong to any organization, he does not belong to any philosophy. In simple, conclusive wards: he does not borrow himself from others. He digs deep within himself and finds his own life juices, finds his own life sources.

What need is there of any path? You are already here – you exist, you are conscious. All that is needed for the basic search is given to you by existence itself.

Look within your consciousness and find the taste of it.

Look within your life and find the eternity of it.

Look within yourself and you will find the holiest, the most sacred temple is your own body – because it enshrines godliness, divineness, all that is beautiful, all that is truthful, all that is valuable.

You are asking, "What guides the rebel?"

That's the beauty of the rebel – that he does not need a guide. He is his own guide, he is his own path, he is his awn philosophy, he is his own future. It is a declaration that "I am all that I need and existence is my home. I am not a stranger here."

CHAPTER 15

An Enlightened Rebel Will
Shake The Thrones Of Power

Beloved Osho,
What is the difference between the rebel and the
enlightened one?
Is it possible to be a real rebel without being
enlightened?

IT IS POSSIBLE to be a rebel without being enlightened.
It is also possible to be enlightened without being a
rebel. But both will be halfhearted. Something will be
missing, something which is very essential. It will be
almost like a corpse – the soul is missing.

A rebel who is not enlightened is living in blindness,
unconsciousness, darkness. He does not know what is
right and what is not right – he has no clarity of vision.
He cannot open up other people's hearts for the birth
of a new humanity – he himself is not born yet. His
rebelliousness is nothing but a kind of thinking in his
mind.

He is a revolutionary thinker, he is a philosopher,
but he does not know exactly what will end this night
and how we are going to bring the dawn... how the
sun will rise, and how the birds will sing again and the
flowers will open. But he can dream, he can think. In
the past there have been many philosophers who have
been accepted as rebels, great rebels, but nothing has
come out of them except some beautiful fragments of
thoughts – unconnected, unscientific, non-pragmatic,
impossible to be transformed into reality.

You must have heard the definition of a philosopher: a blind man, on a dark night, in an unlit house, searching for a black cat which is not there. But the trouble does not end here – there are many who have found it! They gave descriptions of the black cat, and because nobody else has seen it, you cannot refute them either. They don't have any evidence – but neither have you! So whatever these blind philosophers go on saying is accepted without being refuted.

It is not refuted on other accounts, too – because the establishment is not worried about these rebels and their rebellious thinking. They know perfectly well that their thoughts are nothing but soap bubbles; in their deep sleep, they have been chattering.

Mick and Joe are returning home from a tour of some vineyards in Italy, where they have been generously entertained by their hosts. "Mick, is we near the city yet?" asks Joe.

"Yes," answers Mick, "we must be. We are knocking down more people."

"Drive slower, then," says Joe.

"What do you mean, drive slower?" says Mick. "You are driving."

A rebel who is not enlightened is a rebel who is blind – not only blind, but also drunk – and his rebelliousness is a kind of reaction. That is the original meaning of the word "rebel" – fighting against something, fighting back. He can see that something is wrong, something has to be destroyed; his life is not free, so there must be chains on his feet, handcuffs on his hands and they must be broken. He has to free himself. But these are all assumptions.

One thing is certain: he knows misery, he knows suffering; he knows that his humanity has been reduced to almost the same level as animals, that his pride has been destroyed, his dignity has been completely erased. He is aware at least of what has been taken away from him and he starts fighting against it. His rebelliousness is a reaction, negative. It is fighting *against* something, not fighting *for* something.

I would like to add to the meaning of "rebel" a positive side too, which is not there in the dictionaries. The dictionaries are all, without exception, giving only one meaning: fighting back, fighting against. But what is the use of fighting back and fighting against, if you don't have a clear perception – for what? If you don't have a vision of the future, and a better future with more rejoicings, then there is no point in unnecessarily fighting. But the rebel who is not enlightened will remain negative in his approach; hence he will remain half.

The enlightened man who is not a rebel is also in the same way half. He knows what has to be achieved, he knows the potential of man, he knows the faraway distant glories possible to humanity. But he is not ready to fight against the existing society, the existing slavery, all the obstacles and hindrances that are between the future and the present, between the old man and the new man. This kind of enlightened man has existed, and he was worshiped – worshiped by the old people, traditional and orthodox, conventional and rooted in the ancient heritage.

The enlightened man has a vision of a better future, of a better man, but he has not the guts to fight for it, to fight against the traditional, the conventional structure of society and the old mind, conditioned and rotten – because he lives on their charity, he lives on their respect and honor, and worship. He is not courageous enough to renounce all the respectability that they are bestowing upon him; to forget being called a saint and a sage by the rotten old past, and just be a nobody – condemned, perhaps crucified, but fighting against what is wrong, and fighting for that which is right and will be a blessing to all.

So both have been there: the unenlightened rebel and the wise man, enlightened but not rebellious. I want you to understand it very clearly that unless a man is both enlightened and rebellious simultaneously he is not whole. He is incomplete, he is not entire; something is missing. He is not rich, not as rich as he could have been if there was nothing missing in him.

My conception of the enlightened man is that of a rebellious, totally rebellious man. To me rebelliousness and enlightenment have become almost a simultaneous phenomenon, a harmonious unity, an organic whole. Hence I say unto you that I am bringing into the world a new man – a new rebel and a new enlightened being all together in a single person, in each individual.

This synthesis has become absolutely necessary.

The past has seen a Gautam Buddha, utterly enlightened but not rebellious. That's why he was not crucified but worshiped, even by kings, emperors, learned people of his century. There was no fear in the establishment of those days that Gautam Buddha was a danger to them.

I have talked about Bakunin, Bukharin, Camus.

All these are rebellious thinkers, but unenlightened. The society has not crucified them either. The society knows that their words are impotent, that they cannot ignite a wildfire in the hearts of humanity. People will read their books as entertainment. More than that is not possible as far as their writings are concerned; hence the society has not only tolerated them but respected them, rewarded them with great prizes.

My rebel will be not only a philosopher, he will be an experienced, awakened being.

His very presence will threaten all the establishments of the world.

His presence will be a challenge to all that enslaves man and destroys his spirit. His presence will become a great fear in all those who are immensely powerful, but know perfectly well that their power depends on the exploitation of men, on keeping man retarded, on destroying man's intelligence, on not allowing man to have his own individuality, his own original face.

Just a few rebellious enlightened people around the world...and all the thrones of power will start shaking.

I can see not only one Jesus on the cross, I can see thousands of Jesuses on the cross. But their death will be the resurrection of a new humanity, a new consciousness, all over the world. Their life will be a tremendous contribution to beautify this world, and their death will also be an even greater contribution: to give man back his dignity, his humanity, his spirituality.

We need thousands of crosses, and thousands of Jesuses hanging on those crosses. Only then the sleeping humanity perhaps may feel that it is time to get up and *do* something.

CHAPTER 16

You Catch the Flame

Beloved Osho,
You are the true rebel, and You are the new man, and
You are a master midwife, helping to give birth to us.
Since true rebellion is born out of awareness, love,
and meditation, as if it is an alchemy, a living wholeness
unto which we simply need to awaken, how can this
rebellion catch like wildfire?

THE QUESTION IS not how this rebellion can catch like a wildfire. The question is for you to catch the flame, for you to become a rebel. Don't be worried how the world should catch the rebellious spirit. You are the world, every individual is the world.

It happened that Akbar, one of the great emperors of India, had made a beautiful pond. He was bringing the most beautiful swans from the highest lake in the world, Mansarovar in the Himalayas; the greatest and the whitest and the most beautiful swans are born only on that lake. For his palace garden he had made a very vast pond, so those big swans wouldn't feel imprisoned. The pond was almost a lake, big enough that they could enjoy freedom. He was standing and watching the completion of the pond; the pond was made completely of pure white marble.

His prime minister said, "The information has reached us that tomorrow the swans are coming. As a welcome for them, we should fill the pond not with water but with milk. Later on of course we will have to change it into water; but for the welcome, for the first day...."

Akbar said, "But from where to get so much milk?"

The prime minister said, "That's easy. We just have to inform the whole capital that the emperor's garden is receiving swans and, as a welcome to the swans from the Himalayas, he wants their pond, at least for the first day, to be filled with milk. Everybody in the city is requested to bring a bucket of milk."

The capital was large, and if everybody brought one bucket of milk the pond was certainly going to be filled with milk. And who was not going to fulfill the request? In fact it was a joy to join the emperor in welcoming the swans coining from the Himalayas – such a rare variety.

Hindus have always worshiped the swans for their great capacity that if you mix water and milk – perhaps it is a mythological idea – the swan is capable of drinking just the milk and leaving the water. If water and milk are mixed it is almost impossible to separate them, but the swan has that capacity. This must be a mythology – certainly it is a mythology – but it has great significance. It means the man who can separate the unreal from the real, the mortal from the immortal, the mundane from the sacred, the man who can separate sleep from awakening...he is also called *paramhansa*, "the great swan."

The emperor was very happy. But the next day there was a great surprise for the whole palace, because the whole pond was full of water. Everybody in the city had thought, "Just one bucket of water when there will be millions of buckets of milk – who can detect it? You just have to go a little early, when it is dark." So everybody went a little early when it was dark, and everybody poured in water, hoping that everybody else is pouring in milk. Not a single man in the whole capital poured in milk.

You simply think about yourself – your bucket should be full of milk. Don't bother about others.

Everybody has to think about himself. If he is to save his organic unity – his joy in the world and his ecstasy of consciousness, together – he has to become part of the great rebellion I am talking about. This rebellion is going to be the religion of the future. But each individual has to take the responsibility on his own shoulders.

Just think about yourself – that's enough.

And if you become aflame, if people see both Zorba and Buddha in you, you will create a great challenge around yourself for everybody. If you can become so rich on the outside and on the inside, so rich that you can have roots deep in the earth and wings flying in the sky, that you can master matter and consciousness both together – then it will be an invitation and a challenge, and an exciting journey for anybody who comes in contact with you.

Rebellion is always contagious; it is a wildfire.

But you should have the flame.

Then wherever you move, you will go on setting people on fire – people becoming aflame with a new light, with a new vision, with a new idea, and a new conception of man and his future.

An astronaut lands on Mars and comes across a beautiful Martian woman stirring a pot over a flaming fire. "What are you doing?" he asked. "Making babies," she replied.

"That is not how we do it on the earth," he told her.

"How is it done there?" she asked.

"I can't explain, but I can *show* you how – may I?"

"Sure," she said, and he proceeded to show her how it is done. When they had finished she asked, "Where are the babies?"

"Oh," he told her, "they don't come for another nine months." "So," she replied, "why did you stop stirring? Go on stirring, that's how we do it. Until the babies come – go on stirring."

You are asking how this fire can become a wildfire around the earth. Just go on stirring!

CHAPTER 17

The Ultimate Love Affair

Beloved Osho,
What is the path of devotion and does it have a place
in Your vision of the rebel?

DEVOTION IS NOT a path.

You don't have to travel it.

Devotion is a way of merging and melting into existence.

It is not a pilgrimage; it is simply losing all the boundaries that divide you from existence. It is a love affair.

Love is not a path.

Love is a merger with an individual, a deep intimacy of two hearts – so deep that the two hearts start dancing in the same harmony. Although the hearts are two, the harmony is one, the music is one, the dance is one.

What love is between individuals, devotion is between one rebel and the whole existence. He dances in the waves of the ocean, he dances in the dancing trees in the sun, he dances with the stars. His heart responds to the fragrance of flowers, to the song of the birds, to the silences of the night.

Devotion is not a path.

Devotion is the death of the personality.

That which is mortal in you, you drop on your own accord; only the immortal remains, the eternal remains, the deathless remains. And naturally the deathless cannot be separate from the existence – which is deathless, which is always ongoing, knows no beginning, no end.

Devotion is the highest form of love.

It is possible you may love one person, and love becomes so deep that slowly, slowly, the very quality of love changes into devotion. Then that person becomes only a window for you to take a jump into existence.

That is the situation of the master, as far as the rebel is concerned.

For my people I am not a savior, I am not a messiah. I am just a door, a bridge to pass on into the infinite.

India has a very strange city; perhaps in the world there is no other city like it – Fateh-pur Sikri. It was made by great emperor Akbar.

He wanted to make a special city for his capital. The whole city had to be totally fresh, a piece of art, and he would shift the whole capital from Delhi to Fateh-pur Sikri. He was a very demanding man, and it had not to be an ordinary city; every house had to be a palace.

For forty years continuously the city was built – it is surrounded by a beautiful lake – but it was never inhabited. This is the only city in the whole world which has such beautiful palaces, but nobody ever lived there because Akbar died before he could complete the project. The project was too big – to make a whole capital, absolutely fresh and new, out of a special stone, and all the houses, all the roads in a certain pattern with a certain meaning.... Thousands of artists from all over the world were called to work, stone-cutters, masons, architects.

Akbar had perhaps the greatest empire in the whole world in those days. Under Akbar, India was the greatest land, there was immense money, but Akbar spent everything. He wanted the capital to be complete before his death, but seeing that it seemed to be impossible, that the capital would take at least forty years more to be absolutely complete, he decided, "At least while I am alive, half of the capital – particularly the offices of the government and the special people – should move."

A beautiful bridge was made across the lake to join it with the main road; the city was almost a small island inside the lake. Akbar asked his wise people to find a beautiful sentence to be engraved on the main gate of the bridge, to welcome any visitor to the city.

They searched and searched in all the scriptures, in all the literature of the world. It is strange that although they were Mohammedans, they could find a sentence only in the sayings of Jesus which was absolutely suitable, as if it was being said specially to be engraved on the capital of Fateh-pur Sikri. The sentence is, "It is only a bridge. Remember, don't make your house on it. It is a place to pass on."

It is a statement about life. Life is a bridge. Don't make your house on it – it is a place to pass on.

Akbar loved the sentence. It is engraved on Fateh-pur Sikri's main gate. But before any move could happen, he died. His son had been, from the very beginning, against the idea, for the simple reason that the whole treasure had been destroyed and nothing else had been done, only a dead capital had been made – and Delhi was doing perfectly well. There was no need, and in fact he had no money left to continue the project for forty more years, so the project was dropped; nobody ever moved. It became a monument, a great memory of the dream of a great king. But to me the most important thing is the sentence on the bridge.

That's what a master is for a rebel.

That's what love is for a rebel.

For a rebel, love and the master are synonymous.

When his love becomes so deep with the master that he cannot think of himself as separate in any way, love has transformed itself into a new height. That height has been known as devotion.

Devotion is not a path.

Devotion is only a love affair, purified to its ultimate state. Then whomsoever you love becomes a door, a bridge to the universal organic unity, the experience of dissolving in the ocean of your small identity, just like a dewdrop slipping from a lotus leaf.

CHAPTER 18

Take Life As
a Beautiful Joke

Beloved Osho,
What is the secret of a true rebel that allows him to
destroy the old structures, stand up against the whole
world, and still remain non-serious?

THE SECRET IS not much of a secret.

It is an open secret.

The true rebel has an understanding of the
momentariness of life, of the certainty of death; hence
nothing can make him afraid, nothing can make him
compromise. In such a momentary life one is absolutely
able to live without any compromise, and when death is
certain there is no need for compromise at all.

Because life is so short, the rebel can do whatever he
is capable of with his total being – whatever he enjoys
to create and whatever needs to be destroyed for that
creation to happen. He is not destructive; even if he has
to destroy, it is always in the service of creation. And still
he remains…because he is not a reactionary, he has no
complaint against anybody, he remains playful, because
all creativity is playfulness. He is non-serious, because
seriousness is also part of the old man.

The new man, the rebel, has a tremendous sense
of humor. He can laugh in the face of death. While
living, while fighting, while creating or destroying,
he is never serious; he is giggling with joy. He is not a

miserable person — that's what he is revolting against. He wants the whole world to be filled with laughter; he wants to create religions based on laughter as the most fundamental doctrine.

And what is there to be disturbed about, even if the whole world is against you? It really makes you stronger, gives you more nourishment, because it strengthens your conclusions that whatever you are doing is a rebellious act; otherwise the whole world would not be against you.

The very beauty of being a rebel showers one with flowers, because by being a rebel you go to your ultimate heights and to your ultimate depths.

After many years, the ultra-orthodox sect had built their giant computer in Tel Aviv. It was light-years ahead of all other machines, and it had been invented for the purpose of answering one question only. So that fateful day; in fear and anticipation, the question was fed to the mechanical brain, "Is there a God?"

The computer flashed, whirled and out came the answer: "There is *now.*"

The computer is declaring himself God! Now, do you want to take it seriously?

"Goldberg, is it true that you have joined the Catholic church?"

"Yes," said Goldberg, "I joined it last week."

"But," said his friend, "you have always been a Jewish rabbi!"

"I know," said Goldberg, "but I have only got six months to live, and if anybody has got to lose a member, it had better be those buggers."

Take life as a beautiful joke. There is nothing to be serious about.

The late unlamented Heil Hitler was at one time troubled by unusual dreams. He sent for his dream interpreter, who told him the forecast that he would die on a Jewish holiday. "But which one?" asked the apprehensive Fuhrer. "Any day you die will be a Jewish holiday," was the answer.

Just look around life. It is so ridiculous, so humorous. Only people who are blind can be serious; with eyes, it is impossible to be serious.

Harry was fixing his car outside his house. He had the bonnet off, the car up, and his head inside, when a drunk came by. "What is the matter, old man?" the drunk asks Harry. "Piston broke," said Harry. "Ah," commiserated the drunk, "pissed and broke – so am I, so am I."

Just be watchful, look all around and you will be surprised how many beautiful things you are missing.

"Harry," asks his wife, "if we had a four minute nuclear warning, what would you do?"

"Make love to you," answered Harry.

"Yes," said his wife, "but what about the other three minutes?"

Information About
The Original Audio Series

Books by Osho are transcriptions from discourses given before a live audience. All Osho discourses have been published in full as books and are also available as original audio recordings. Information about the audio recordings and the complete text archive can be found at the OSHO Library at www.osho.com.

About the Author

Osho defies categorization, reflecting everything from the individual quest for meaning to the most urgent social and political issues facing society today. His books are not written but are transcribed from recordings of extemporaneous talks given over a period of thirty-five years. Osho has been described by *The Sunday Times* in London as one of the "1000 Makers of the 20th Century" and by *Sunday Mid-Day* in India as one of the ten people – along with Gandhi, Nehru and Buddha – who have changed the destiny of India.

Osho has a stated aim of helping to create the conditions for the birth of a new kind of human being, characterized as "Zorba the Buddha" – one whose feet are firmly on the ground, yet whose hands can touch the stars. Running like a thread through all aspects of Osho's talks and meditations is a vision that encompasses both the timeless wisdom of the East and the highest potential of Western science and technology.

He is synonymous with a revolutionary contribution to the science of inner transformation and an approach to meditation which specifically addresses the accelerated pace of contemporary life. The unique OSHO® Active Meditations™ are designed to allow the release of accumulated stress in the body and mind so that it is easier to be still and experience the thought-free state of meditation.

OSHO International Meditation Resort

Every year the OSHO® International Meditation Resort™ welcomes thousands of people from over 100 countries who come to enjoy and participate in its unique atmosphere of meditation and celebration. The 28-acre meditation resort is located about 100 miles southeast of Mumbai (Bombay), in Pune, India, in a tree-lined residential area, set against a backdrop of bamboo groves and wild jasmine, peacocks and waterfalls, The basic approach of the meditation resort is that of Zorba the Buddha: living in awareness, with a capacity to celebrate everything in life. Many visitors come to just be, to allow themselves the luxury of doing nothing. Others choose to participate in a wide variety of courses and sessions that support moving toward a more joyous and less stressful life, by combining methods of self-understanding with awareness techniques. These courses are offered through OSHO® Multiversity™ and take place in a pyramid complex next to the famous OSHO® Teerth Park. ™

People can choose to practice various meditation methods, both active and passive, from a daily schedule that begins at six o'clock in the morning. Early each evening there is a meditation event that moves from dance to silent sitting, using Osho's recorded talks as an opportunity to experience inner silence without effort.

Facilities include tennis courts, a gym, sauna, Jacuzzi, a nature-shaped Olympic-sized swimming pool, classes in Zen archery, Tai chi, Chi gong, Yoga and a multitude of bodywork sessions.

The kitchen serves international gourmet vegetarian meals, made with organically grown produce. The nightlife is alive with friends dining under the stars, and with music and dancing.

Online bookings for accommodation at the OSHO® Guesthouse which is inside the meditation resort can be made through the website below or by sending an email to: guesthouse@osho.com

Online tours of the meditation resort, how to get there, and program information can be found at: http://www.osho.com/resort

For detailed information to participate in this meditation resort please contact:

OSHO INTERNATIONAL MEDITATION RESORT
17 Koregaon Park, Pune—411001, MS, India
Phone: +91-20-66019999 Fax:+91- 20-66019990
Email: resortinfo@osho.net Website: http://www.osho.com

Books by Osho in English

EARLY DISCOURSES AND WRITINGS
A Cup of Tea
Dimensions Beyond The Known
From Sex to Super-consciousness
The Great Challenge
Hidden Mysteries
I Am The Gate
The Inner Journey
Psychology of the Esoteric
Seeds of Wisdom

MEDITATION
The Voice of Silence
And Now and Here (Vol 1 & 2)
In Search of the Miraculous (Vol 1 &.2)
Meditation: The Art of Ecstasy
Meditation: The First and Last Freedom
The Path of Meditation
The Perfect Way
Yaa-Hoo! The Mystic Rose

BUDDHA AND BUDDHIST MASTERS
The Book of Wisdom
The Dhammapada: The Way of the Buddha (Vol 1-12)
The Diamond Sutra
The Discipline of Transcendence (Vol 1-4)
The Heart Sutra

INDIAN MYSTICS
Enlightenment: The Only Revolution (Ashtavakra)
Showering Without Clouds   (Sahajo)
The Last Morning Star (Daya)
The Song of Ecstasy (Adi Shankara)

BAUL MYSTICS
The Beloved (Vol 1 & 2)

KABIR
The Divine Melody
Ecstasy: The Forgotten Language
The Fish in the Sea is Not Thirsty
The Great Secret
The Guest
The Path of Love
The Revolution

JESUS AND CHRISTIAN MYSTICS
Come Follow to You (Vol 1-4)
I Say Unto You (Vol 1 & 2)
The Mustard Seed
Theologia Mystica

JEWISH MYSTICS
The Art of Dying
The True Sage

WESTERN MYSTICS
Guida Spirituale (Desiderata)
The Hidden Harmony (Heraclitus)
The Messiah (Vol 1 & 2)   (Commentaries on Khalil Gibran's The
    Prophet)
The New Alchemy: To Turn You On
    (Commentaries on Mabel Collins' Light on the Path)
Philosophia Perennis (Vol 1 & 2)
    (The Golden Verses of Pythagoras)
Zarathustra: A God That Can Dance
Zarathustra: The Laughing Prophet (Commentaries on Nietzsche's
    Thus Spake Zarathustra)

SUFISM
Just Like That
Journey to the Heart
The Perfect Master (Vol 1 & 2)
The Secret
Sufis: The People of the Path (Vol 1 & 2)

Unio Mystica (Vol 1 & 2)
The Wisdom of the Sands(Vol 1 & 2)

TANTRA
Tantra: The Supreme Understanding
The Tantra Experience
The Royal Song of Saraha (same as Tantra Vision, Vol 1)
The Tantric Transformation
The Royal Song of Saraha (same as Tantra Vision, Vol 2)
The Book of Secrets: Vigyan Bhairav Tantra

THE UPANISHADS
Behind a Thousand Names (Nirvana Upanishad)
Heartbeat of the Absolute (Ishavasya Upanishad)
I Am That (Isa Upanishad)
The Message Beyond Words (Kathopanishad)
Philosophia Ultima   (Mandukya Upanishad)
The Supreme Doctrine   (Kenopanishad)
Finger Pointing to the Moon (Adhyatma Upanishad)
That Art Thou   (Sarvasar Upanishad, Kaivalya Upanishad, Adhyatma
    Upanishad)
The Ultimate Alchemy, Vol 1&2 (Atma Pooja Upanishad Vol 1 &2)
Vedanta: Seven Steps to Samadhi (Akshaya Upanishad)
Flight of the Alone to the Alone (Kaivalya Upanishad)

TAO
The Empty Boat
The Secret of Secrets
Tao:The Golden Gate (Vol 1&2)
Tao:The Pathless Path (Vol 1&2)
Tao: The Three Treasures (Vol 1-4)
When the Shoe Fits

YOGA
The Path of Yoga (previously Yoga: The Alpha and the Omega (Vol 1)
Yoga: The Alpha and the Omega (Vol 2-10)

ZEN AND ZEN MASTERS
Ah, This!
Ancient Music in the Pines

And the Flowers Showered
A Bird on the Wing
Bodhidharma: The Greatest Zen Master
Communism and Zen Fire, Zen Wind
Dang Dang Doko Dang
The First Principle
God is Dead: Now Zen is the Only Living Truth
The Grass Grows By Itself
The Great Zen Master Ta Hui
Hsin Hsin Ming: The Book of Nothing
I Celebrate Myself: God is No Where, Life is Now Here
Kyozan: A True Man of Zen
Nirvana: The Last Nightmare
No Mind: The Flowers of Eternity
No Water, No Moon
One Seed Makes the Whole Earth Green
Returning to the Source
The Search: Talks on the 10 Bulls of Zen
A Sudden Clash of Thunder
The Sun Rises in the Evening
Take it Easy (Vol 1 & 2)
This Very Body the Buddha
Walking in Zen, Sitting in Zen
The White Lotus
Yakusan: Straight to the Point of Enlightenment
Zen Manifesto : Freedom From Oneself
Zen: The Mystery and the Poetry of the Beyond
Zen: The Path of Paradox (Vol 1, 2 & 3)
Zen: The Special Transmission
Zen Boxed Sets
The World of Zen (5 vol.)
Live Zen
This. This. A Thousand Times This
Zen: The Diamond Thunderbolt
Zen: The Quantum Leap from Mind to No-Mind
Zen: The Solitary Bird, Cuckoo
of the Forest
Zen: All The Colors Of The Rainbow (5 vol.)

The Buddha: The Emptiness of the Heart
The Language of Existence
The Miracle
The Original Man
Turning In

OSHO: On the Ancient Masters of Zen (7 volumes)*

Dogen: The Zen Master
Hyakujo: The Everest of Zen–
With Basho's haikus
Isan: No Footprints in the Blue Sky
Joshu: The Lion's Roar
Ma Tzu: The Empty Mirror
Nansen: The Point Of Departure
Rinzai: Master of the Irrational
Each volume is also available individually.

RESPONSES TO QUESTIONS

Be Still and Know
Come, Come, Yet Again Come
The Goose is Out
The Great Pilgrimage: From Here to Here
Invitation
My Way: The Way of the White Clouds
Nowhere to Go But In
The Razor's Edge
Walk Without Feet, Fly Without Wings and Think Without Mind
The Wild Geese and the Water
Zen: Zest, Zip, Zap and Zing
From Bondage To Freedom
From Darkness to Light
From Death To Deathlessness
From the False to the Truth
From Unconsciousness to Consciousness
The Rajneesh Bible (Vol 2-4)
Beyond Enlightenment (Talks in Bombay)
Beyond Psychology (Talks in Uruguay)
Light on the Path (Talks in the Himalayas)
The Path of the Mystic (Talks in Uruguay)

Sermons in Stones (Talks in Bombay)
Socrates Poisoned Again After 25 Centuries (Talks in Greece)
The Sword and the Lotus (Talks in the Himalayas)
The Transmission of the Lamp (Talks in Uruguay)

OSHO'S VISION FOR THE WORLD
The Golden Future
The Hidden Splendor
The New Dawn
The Rebel
The Rebellious Spirit

THE MANTRA SERIES
Hari Om Tat Sat
Om Mani Padme Hum
Om Shantih Shantih Shantih
Sat-Chit-Anand
Satyam-Shivam-Sundram

PERSONAL GLIMPSES
Books I Have Loved
Glimpses of a Golden Childhood
Notes of a Madman

INTERVIEWS WITH THE WORLD PRESS
The Man of Truth: A Majority of One

For any information about OSHO Books, please contact:
OSHO Media International
17 Koregaon Park, Pune – 411001, MS, India
Phone: +91-20-66019999 Fax: +91-20-66019990
E-mail: distribution@osho.net
Website: http://www.osho.com

FULL
CIRCLE

Full Circle is a distinguished publisher of non-fiction, and classic and contemporary fiction. Known for quality publishing and production, Full Circle continues its commitment towards providing good reading at great value.

We are dedicated towards creating a peaceful and harmonious inner and outer world ever mindful of our connection with the divine human spirit.

Our fine books are available at leading bookstores across the country and the Full Circle Bookstores below:

Bookstores

23, Khan Market, 1st & 2nd Floor
New Delhi-110003 Tel: 24655641/2/3

N-16, Greater Kailash Part I Market
New Delhi-110048 Tel: 29245641/2/3/4

Number 8, Nizamuddin East Market
New Delhi-110013 Tel: 41826124/5

Editorial Office

J-40, Jorbagh Lane, New Delhi-110003
Tel: +011-24621011

contact@fullcirclebooks.in • www.fullcirclebooks.in

Full Circle Books by
OSHO

Die O Yogi Die

Gorakh is one of the four people whom Osho calls "the foundation stones of Indian mysticism". Gorakh is direct and to the point, earthy, an "unpolished diamond" who doesn't allow any detours or side-stepping on the path to self-realization.

This book is about the death of the ego and the practical steps everyone can take to live a full, aware and joyful life.

Behind a Thousand Names

Osho loves the Nirvan Upanishads because it is so revolutionary – revolutionary because it insists that the only way to experience true awareness is to go beyond all systems of morality. Maybe this startling message is the reason why Osho's commentary on this Upanishad is the first that has ever been made.

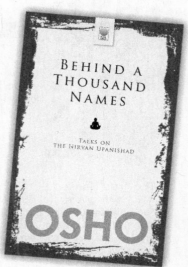

Available at all leading bookstores.

Full Circle Books by
OSHO

Won't You Join the Dance
That's what I teach, trust your intelligence, trust your own heart, its feelings — and even if sometimes it looks crazy to follow those feelings, go with them.

Truth Simply Is...
In this book, Osho takes us step-by-step through Sufism – How to arrive at the gentle meaning of Sufism and learn to nourish ourselves by applying it to our daily life.

The Secret
This is not really a book. It is more of a dance. And not an ordinary dance. It is Sufi Whirlwind from the heart. This book is a song, a remembrance, an embrace, a longing — *zhikr*... for that secret moment.

The True Name
Talks on the Wisdom of Guru Nanak Dev
Spoken with authority, clarity, sharpness and humor, his insights address both the timeless and timely concerns that tend to escape our notice in the clamor and overload of daily life.

Available at all leading bookstores.

Join the
World Wisdom
Book Club

GET THE BEST OF WORLD LITERATURE IN THE COMFORT OF YOUR HOME AT FABULOUS DISCOUNTS!

Benefits of the Book Club

Wherever in the world you are, you can receive the best of books at your doorstep.

- Receive FABULOUS DISCOUNTS by mail or at the **FULL CIRCLE** Bookstores in Delhi.

- Receive Exclusive Invitations to attend events being organized by **FULL CIRCLE**.

- Receive a FREE copy of the club newsletter — The World Wisdom Review — every month.

- Get UP TO 10% OFF.

Join Now!

It's simple. Just fill in the coupon overleaf and mail it to us at the address below:

FULL CIRCLE
J-40, Jorbagh Lane, New Delhi-110003
Tel: 24620063, 24621011 • Fax: 24645795
E-mail: contact@fullcirclebooks.in *www.fullcirclebooks.in*

Yes, I would like to be a member of the

World Wisdom Book Club

Name ☐ Mr ☐ Mrs ☐ Ms..

Mailing Address...

....

....

City.................................... Pin.......................

Phone............................ Fax............................

E-mail...

Profession............................ D.O.B.....................

Areas of Interest...

....

Mail this form to:
The World Wisdom Book Club
J-40, Jorbagh Lane, New Delhi-110003
Tel: 24620063, 24621011 • Fax: 24645795
E-mail: contact@fullcirclebooks.in ***www.fullcirclebooks.in***

THE REBEL